P9-DTP-950

COLORS OF AFRICA

COLORS OF
AFRICA

JAMES KILGO

with illustrations by the author

THE UNIVERSITY OF GEORGIA PRESS

ATHENS AND LONDON

Published by the University of Georgia Press

Athens, Georgia 30602

© 2003 by James Kilgo

All rights reserved

Designed by Sandra Strother Hudson

Set in Minion with Pietra display by Graphic Composition, Inc.

Printed and bound by Maple-Vail

The paper in this book meets the guidelines for permanence and

durability of the Committee on Production Guidelines

for Book Longevity of the Council on Library Resources.

Printed in the United States of America

07 06 05 04 03 C 5 4 3 2 1

Library of Congress Cataloging-in-Publication Data

Kilgo, James, 1941–

Colors of Africa / James Kilgo, with illustrations by the author.

p. cm.

ISBN 0-8203-2500-7 (alk. paper)

1. Luangwa River Valley (Zambia and Mozambique)—Description and travel.

2. Natural history—Luangwa River Valley (Zambia and Mozambique) 3. Safaris—

Luangwa River Valley (Zambia and Mozambique) 4. Kilgo, James, 1941–

—Journeys—Luangwa River Valley (Zambia and Mozambique) I. Title.

DT3140.L83 K55 2003

916.89404'42—dc21   2002013117

British Library Cataloging-in-Publication Data available

To Susan Aiken and Coleman Barks
and in memory of Stan Lindberg,
who aided and abetted.

I have spent four weeks in the happy hunting grounds and have just emerged from the depths of the great wide open spaces, from the life of prehistoric times, today just as it was a thousand years ago, from meeting with the great beasts of prey, which enthrall one, which obsess one so that one feels that lions are all that one lives for—strengthened by the air of the high mountain region, tanned by its sun, filled with its wild, free magnificent beauty in heat-dazzling days, in great clear moonlit nights. I must humbly apologize to those hunters whose delight in the chase I failed to understand. There is nothing in the world to equal it—

ISAK DINESEN, *Letters from Africa*

At such times, and myriad others perhaps, we know that we live our way deeply in the present, only to discover that we are invaded by the Eternal.

HOWARD THURMAN, *The Inward Journey*

CONTENTS

COLORS OF AFRICA

THE ZEBRA lay on the blackened ground, its legs and the underside of its belly smudged by ash. It was about the size of a pony. The pattern of its stripes had never occurred on any zebra before. The man who had killed it wondered at the colors of the muzzle, soot black around the mouth and nostrils, velvety brown ochre on the sides of the nose. He asked the professional hunter if the brown was typical—he had thought zebras were simply black and white.

No, said the PH. Most muzzles were all black, but some had brown like this one.

The smell of the zebra was strong, like the smell of horses.

The PH squatted in the ash and stroked the muscled neck. "These are the colors of Africa," he said.

The blood that flowed from the zebra's mouth was dark red and clotted.

INTRODUCTION

I WENT ON SAFARI in Africa in the spring of the year 2000, in the Luangwa River valley of Zambia. Our camp stood on the east bank of the river not far downstream from where David Livingstone crossed in his search for the source of the Nile. For three weeks we lived in the bush and slept under a deep night sky. At first light the weather was cool and clear. As we drank our morning coffee, vervet monkeys in the branches overhead began to stir, seeking the warmth of the sun. During the day we walked among giraffe, elephant, and zebra, and Cape turtledoves called from dawn to dark. Twice a day we ate wild meat. In bed at night I could see unfamiliar constellations through an opening between the wall and the roof; I listened to hippos and hyenas, and smoke from the mopani wood campfire drifted through the grass walls of the hut. The clock stopped, and I was closer than I had ever come to the world as it is made. Then one day we packed our gear, reset our watches, and returned to the Northern Hemisphere.

We came home with fifteen rolls of film and eighteen hours of videotape—freeze-dried memories to be framed, hung on walls, or played on TV screens—but it has been a year now and my memories have not yet accepted frames. Instead of hanging obediently in a gallery alongside recollections of other trips, they insist on breaking out, like animals that won't tolerate a fence, like the engraved and painted animals of Pleistocene art that move across unframed faces of rock, dynamic, overlapping, polychromatic, and out of all proportion to the time and space of nature.

KING SOLOMON, like his father David, was a poet. The Old Testament book of First Kings reports that "he spake of trees, from the cedar tree that is in Lebanon even unto the hyssop that springeth out of the wall:

he spake also of beasts, and of fowl, and of creeping things, and of fishes" (1 Kings 4:33). What I love about that verse is the absence of any apology or explanation of Solomon's choice of landscape and animals as subject. It reminds me of the cave paintings and rock art of Paleolithic man. The major decorated caves of southern Europe— Altamira, Lascaux, Les Trois Freres, and Chauvet—and the granite shelters of southern Africa do nothing to explain themselves beyond suggesting that our ancestors were captivated by animals. Thirty thousand years ago at Chauvet, people anatomically and psychologically like us crept into the deepest reaches of a pitch-black tunnel that stank of bears; by the light of torches they ground iron oxide into red ochre and burnt wood into charcoal powder; against damp walls they erected ladders and scaffolding; and then they drew and painted and engraved, sometimes in proportions larger than life, the great beasts they lived among—the ones they hunted and the ones that hunted them.

The walls and vaulted ceilings of the painted caves are crowded with animals, vibrant herds of horses, bison, bulls, reindeer, lions, and rhinos—a Pleistocene bestiary emerging from crevices in the rock as from the hand of God, pouring over bulges, spilling down long panels. People who have been admitted to the caves report a sense of the sacred. They say they felt as though they had entered a sanctuary.

Radiocarbon dating indicates that cave painting in southern Europe spanned a period of twenty-five thousand years, dying out in the late Magdalenian, twelve thousand years ago. At about the time it ceased, aboriginal peoples of southern Africa began to represent their visions of animals on the walls of shallow rock shelters. There is great diversity in the rock art of Africa, but wherever it occurs, at whatever antiquity, its most striking feature, especially in contrast to the European cave paintings, is the presence of humans. The people who made these drawings included themselves. The figures are usually shown in association with animals—elephant, buffalo, eland, and kudu—typically hunting or dancing, but whereas in many instances the animals are rendered in impressive naturalistic detail, the humans are highly stylized.

The presence of humans is only one, though for me the most striking, of many differences between European cave painting and African rock art, but for all those differences they prompt the same questions—not only who, when, and how, but most insistently, why?

Since the first European discoveries of Stone Age art in the late nineteenth century, anthropologists and ethnologists have struggled to explain it, an effort characterized by insight and controversy and, as new discoveries come to light, a constant need to revise and update. An early theory held that the drawings were made simply in celebration of the beauty of animals, art for art's sake, like the poetry of King Solomon. A more persistent interpretation saw the images as attempts at sympathetic hunting magic, a ritualistic means of evoking the prey animal as a way of exercising control over it. Yet another argued that the animals are totems of human attributes and gender, a projection of order and purpose in emerging human communities. More recently, two leading authorities on Paleolithic art—Jean Clotte of France and David Lewis-Williams of South Africa—have agreed that both the painted caves and the decorated rock shelters are results of shamanic activity—a rendering of the shaman's underworld encounter with spirit animals.

It seems unlikely that any single purpose can account for a practice that lasted twenty-five thousand years, but a statement by the novelist Reynolds Price recognizes the essential nature of cave art: "And to glance again at paleolithic cave painting and the hundreds of exquisitely engraved stones and bones is to confront their radiant numinosity—something transcendent in beast, man, and nature is implored and entreated with delight and reverence." Each compelling image explains what Claude Levi-Strauss meant when he said that "some animals are good to think."

The hunter-shaman-artist musters all his courage to enter the cave. The walls that enclose him become thinner and thinner membranes between himself and the spirit world where animals have their true lives. Unable to see with his eyes, he passes his palms over the damp, uneven surfaces. He begins to feel the shoulderings and nosings of horned creatures and to smell through stone the stench of meat eaters. And then he dips his brush into a clay pot of pigment.

Part One

AFRICA, BY GOD

Walking down to the forest after telling these poor people, for the first time in their lives, that the Son of God had so loved them as to come down from heaven to save them, I observed many regiments of black soldier-ants returning from their marauding expeditions.

DAVID LIVINGSTONE, *Missionary Travels*

In the quietest parts of the forest there is heard a faint but distinct hum, which tells of insect joy. One may see many whisking about in the clear sunshine in patches among the green glancing leaves; but there are invisible myriads working with never-tiring mandibles on leaves, and stalks, and beneath the soil. They are all brimful of enjoyment. Indeed the universality of organic life may be called a mantle of happy existence encircling the world, and imparts the idea of its being caused by the consciousness of our benignant Father's smile on all the works of His hands.

DAVID LIVINGSTONE, *Missionary Travels*

I

▼▼▼▼▼

IT MUST HAVE STARTED with a book, this matter of Africa. Somewhere back in childhood lies a volume, Victorian by the heft and color, library by the smell. I don't remember the author or the title, though I think *Africa* was in it, and I doubt that I read much of the text, but the illustrations—black and white wood engravings, protected by sheets of tissue—imparted scenes of vibrant color that permeated my imagination.

Fifty years later I had reason to say to my children, "If I should not wake up tomorrow morning I want y'all to know that I have done pretty much everything I set out to do." Then even to my surprise I blurted out, "Except go to Africa." I smiled in an effort to make a joke of what I had said. I did not want them to think that Africa actually ranked as a major goal of my life. But maybe it mattered more than I had realized. Books and movies about exploration and safari had continued from childhood to ignite my sensibility. I had never outgrown Hemingway or tired of Isak Dinesen, and for most of my life I had dreamed: *some day.* But the instant I blurted out "Africa," I realized that the time had passed; somewhere during my middle years I had quietly surrendered to the obstacles that stood in the way of making such a trip—lack of money, lack of time, political changes in East Africa, and, most recently, uncertain health. What I was left with was a lively romantic sense of an Africa that no longer existed, either in fact or for me.

Two years later, a stranger stepped out of a crowd and asked me to go to Zambia with him. He wasn't a perfect stranger, any more than I was to him. We were both participating as team members on a weekend retreat sponsored by our church denomination. He stuck out his hand and introduced himself. Steve Ebbert. Oh, I thought, so this is Steve Ebbert, the man who owned the office park where my wife worked. She had told me that he had heads of African animals mounted on the walls of his office, but I was not impressed. Though I had once been a hunter myself, I had little sympathy for big-game trophy collectors. Besides that, Ebbert was a developer, for which I had even less. Yet here we were at the same place on the same weekend—a coincidence that suggested that we might agree on at least a few things. To make conversation, I asked if he was planning another trip to Africa.

Steve is a short man—five feet two inches tall—but when he gripped my hand, I felt his strength. Broad in the shoulders, powerful in his forearms, he was lean and fit, and he generated a field of energy that almost buzzed. "That's what I wanted to talk with you about," he said.

Steve had booked a twenty-one-day safari in Zambia. He would be hunting leopard, lion, and buffalo as well as plains game, and he could take two nonhunting observers. He had already enlisted a college student to operate a video camera. They were to leave in two months. "Do you want to go with us?"

I refused to let myself take him seriously. The cost might be prohibitive, and even should it not, he and I might well prove incompatible. I knew nothing about this man. More to the point, since it was his safari, he knew nothing about me. Three weeks together in the bush might turn out to be a misery to us both. Why would he take such a risk? "What would you want me to do?" I asked.

"Write," he said.

Write what? I wondered. If he was looking to hire a hack to celebrate his exploits in an outdoor magazine, he would have to look elsewhere.

He must have seen the question on my face. "I read *Deep Enough for Ivorybills*," he said. "I'd like to see you take a shot at Africa."

He was referring to my first book, a nonfiction narrative about my days of hunting and especially the fellowship I had enjoyed with other hunters. If he had read that he knew more about me than I had suspected, for the book made it clear that I had been selective about the men I hunted with. If he had really liked it, there was a chance that we might find common ground after all. "I'll go," I said.

Steve laughed. "Don't you need to talk to Jane first?"

"No, I'll go. I'm going." I wanted to make that clear lest he change his mind.

Steve laughed again and shook my hand. The deal was done.

MY CHIEF CONCERN was my health. Seven years earlier, at the age of fifty-one, I had been diagnosed with prostate cancer. After a radical prostatectomy, my doctor told me that the tumor had all but broken through the prostate capsule; in this situation there was a thirty percent chance of recurrence. A year later a biopsy detected residual malignancy in the prostatic area. The indicated treatment was external beam radiation. That turned out to be effective for about eighteen months. When the cancer recurred again, my doctors recommended hormone therapy. Monthly injections of the drug blocked the production of testosterone, depriving any lesions of the fuel prostate cancer needs. As expected, it also deprived me of some of the happier effects of testosterone, including stamina and muscle mass, which had never been impressive in the best of times. Until the second recurrence, I had believed that I would be cured, but after that I had to live with the knowledge that my cancer would someday become hormone resistant, that it would "learn" to grow without the fuel of testosterone.

From the time of diagnosis I had received strong support from friends and family. My wife, Jane, as well as several other people, had assured me that God was going to heal me. I didn't understand the mystery of divine healing—why some are healed and others aren't—I still don't—but I knew these people, and there was nothing glib or fraudulent about any of them. Passages from the Bible, especially Psalm 27, that until now had been merely great poetry seemed suddenly to glow, as though I were the reader for whom it was written, and I was comforted. But I could not sustain those flights of faith. When my legs and hips began to hurt and unfamiliar aches visited parts of my body that had never bothered me before, gravity prevailed and peace departed. I thought of others who had been prayed for and died, a six-year-old child who had lived across the street, and through the small nighttime hours when I couldn't sleep, I lay awake listening to dreadful things nosing around the door. But there was Jane sleeping peacefully at my side, breathing deeply in and out, and her very exhalations seemed prayers of supplication and thanksgiving.

Even so, cancer altered the landscape of my personal future and discolored my sense of who I was. If I bought a tool or an article of clothing or new tires for my truck, I wondered if the purchase would outlast me. After thirty-three years of teaching English at the University of Georgia, I retired. I stopped making plans for trips more than six months in advance, and slowly, month by month, as I came more and more to live from one checkup to the next, cancer invaded my psyche as it had my body. Without realizing that I was doing it, I had begun to use illness as an excuse to withdraw from activities that had helped shape my life, especially hunting and fishing. The process was gradual, allowing me time to convince myself that my decision was a matter of ethics—say, a heightened sensitivity to the holiness of life—but honesty forced me to admit that ethics had little to do with it. I had long since settled to my satisfaction the question of killing animals, and I had accepted the consequences. The truth is that I was crawling into a hole, like a wounded animal, to spend my diminished energy on getting well or being sick. Giving up hunting, and later my retirement from the University of Georgia, were merely indicative of a larger resignation.

That's what Steve Ebbert's invitation saved me from. I'm not sure I would have said yes to any other destination, but Africa had the sound of life. A mind-body therapist had once suggested to me that pain in the hips and groin might be a symptom of a person's sense of having nowhere to go, no future to enter. Whether that was true or not, aches and twinges I had experienced intermittently for years disappeared. I found new energy and began working out, walking three miles or more a day through the hills of the Georgia piedmont. I wanted to prepare myself to receive as much of Africa as I could hold.

II
▼▼▼▼▼

YOU CAN'T TELL PEOPLE you're going to Africa without being asked to explain the circumstances. Sooner or later I had to say, "hunting safari," and when I did the barometric pressure in the room usually underwent a change. You could feel it. Disapproval ranged from a politely raised eyebrow to sad disappointment that I would do such a thing to harsh denunciation. "I'm not going to be hunting myself," I would add, quickly protesting the innocence of my intentions. "I used to hunt, but it's been ten years since I killed a deer. I'm just going as an observer, to write and take pictures." But that self-defense made no difference to impassioned antihunting people. One young woman, a former graduate student of mine, chided me harshly for even accompanying a hunter, as though I was aiding and abetting criminal activity. "Take pictures of what?" she demanded. "Carnage?"

A change has occurred over the last twenty years in the sensibility of Americans concerning the issue of hunting, and it is more extensive than I had realized. In the early 1970s an Athens newspaper printed a photograph of a man, who happened to be a friend of mine, posing with a moose he had shot in Alaska. A few days later a clipping of the photo appeared on the bulletin board of the church we attended. As far as I could tell, it provoked no negative reaction. Try posting such a picture in a church these days. Try printing it in a newspaper even.

Not long before we were to leave, friends invited Jane and me to dinner in their home. Among the other guests was a young man from France, a student at the university. Inevitably, someone mentioned my impending trip, and the tape began to play. "How can an educated, civilized person defend something as barbaric as hunting?" the Frenchman wanted to know. Our hosts' elegant table was no place for a discussion that showed every sign of escalating into heated argument, but I could not refrain from pointing out that he was even at that moment enjoying a serving of chicken, a creature whose feet had never touched the ground, whose beak had been burned off while it was still alive, and whose throat had been sliced as it hung by its feet from a conveyor belt. He readily granted the necessity of animals being slaughtered to provide food but argued that there is a great difference between the meatpacking industry and what he called sport hunting. What troubled his puritanical soul was hunters taking pleasure in killing. Sport hunting, he said, made him sick.

Instead of arguing the point, at which I have never been effective, I told the young man a story. Back in the days when I had hunted in a club in South Carolina, our custom at the table each night was to ask the men who had been successful that day to tell what happened. One evening my friend Jeff Carter said he had a story. We were surprised because he had come in from the river swamp without a deer, but the hunt master said, "Tell it," and Jeff pushed back from the table. He was a man of prodigious girth, in the neighborhood of three hundred pounds, but he was spry enough to mount a horse or to climb into a tree stand. He knew what he was doing in the woods, and often enough he killed a deer, but he did not consider himself an exceptional hunter. That day, though, he had felt unusually alert—all eyes and ears—and from the moment he entered the swamp his measured step was closely attuned to the heart of the game. He came to a thicket of switch cane, the stalks taller than he was, and eased through it. From time to time he stopped, by instinct rather than conscious intent. He felt utterly unaware of himself, he said. There was no wind. In the stillness he could hear deer crunching acorns. Directly, he spied movement—a flicking tail, a twitching ear—and slowly he became aware of deer all around him in the dense thicket. Then, a young spike buck appeared at his side. Jeff had neither seen nor heard it approach—it was just there, casually eating acorns as it moved past him. Jeff had only to reach out his hand, palm down, and stroke the deer's back. The canebrake erupted—more deer than Jeff had had any notion of—but he had claimed his buck. He told us that it was the greatest hunt of his life.

"And that," I told the young man, "is one of the best hunting stories I've ever read or heard, and I truly believe that it could have happened only to a hunter, to someone who has mastered not just the skill of stalking but the discipline of inner stillness. It was one of those moments that seems to occur outside of time, that comes as a gift. Jeff said you could almost call it holy. But what I want you to understand is that the experience did not affect his desire to kill a deer the next day."

"So you are asking me to believe that a hunter would rather touch a deer than shoot it?"

"No," I said, "just that that hunter did, at that moment."

THE ATTITUDE that set Jeff Carter apart from many people who hunt is called natural piety—a sense of wonder, a capacity for appreciation, a respect for wild creatures and the country they inhabit. It manifests itself in the choices the hunter makes, in the language he uses to talk about the experience, and in the way he acts when the hunt is over. "My bearing must not shame your quitting life," say the hunters in William Faulkner's fiction. They understood that spilling blood in order to eat involves mystery and must not be done wantonly. I had never been comfortable hunting with men who lacked such understanding, and I hadn't been able to tell yet whether Steve Ebbert did or not.

One day soon after the retreat Steve invited me to lunch with him and Stuart McLean, the college student who would handle the video camera. They had known each other for several years, since the time Stuart began attending a Sunday school class that Steve taught. While still in high school, Stuart had expressed interest in learning to hunt, and Steve had taken him on as a protégé, sacrificing at least a year of independent hunting on his own. By now they had developed a close friendship, though from what I could see the chemistry was unusual. Steve's temperament, though good-natured, was high-octane, brash and opinionated. Stuart, on the other hand, was soft-spoken and deferential, a composed, well-mannered young man. Yet he was as devoted to his mentor as a boy to his favorite uncle. They were buddies. From their point of view, I began to realize, I was the wild card. If I didn't know what I had gotten myself into, neither did they.

Toward the end of April, Steve proposed that the three of us go turkey hunting—a trial run to see how we worked together in the woods—but turkey hunting is not a team sport and we heard no birds anyway. What I did hear was Steve's story. After the hunt, when Stuart had left to go to class and Steve and I sat sharing cups of coffee in the peculiar intimacy of the cab of a pickup, he started talking.

He had grown up in the sixties on the wrong side of Baton Rouge, he began. During his teens he ran wild, smoked dope, and stayed in trouble. Managing somehow to graduate from high school, he enrolled at an agricultural junior college in south Georgia, leaving his misspent youth in Louisiana.

"Did you hunt at all in high school?" I asked.

"I started rabbit hunting when I was thirteen. My stepfather didn't hunt, but the man who lived next door kept rabbit dogs, and he took me. Two years later I had a pack of my own. And squirrels. I hunted squirrels. We used to come in from the woods for breakfast and eat cereal with dead squirrels and rabbits laying on the table.

"My best friend in high school was a hard-core hunter. He would wake me up at 3:00 in the morning tapping on my window because we had an hour and a half to walk to where we wanted to go. We killed our first deer together. We were fifteen. No, sixteen, because I had my twelve-gauge."

Steve paused. "I hate to tell you how it happened. We had been seeing deer in this field in the evening when we came out of the woods so we bought slugs for our shotguns and put on headlamps and went out and waited for them. When it got dark, we shined their eyes. Both me and him shot at the same deer. When we walked up to her, he had hit her in the front legs and I'd gotten her in the back legs. Talk about a sick feeling—man! I shot her in the ribs to put her out of her misery. Didn't even know to shoot her in the head. It was cold—about forty degrees—and steam came out of the hole where I shot her. Then we had to drag her all the way home and hide her in the woods behind the house. My stepfather wore me out about that. The next morning we were skinning her out and cutting up meat when we heard a siren coming down the street. The other guy's parents had told their son-in-law, who was some kind of conservation officer. He wore us out too. But he turned out to be a really great guy. He lectured us on hunting ethics. We later became good friends."

After two years at the south Georgia junior college, Steve entered the forestry school at the University of Georgia. Following graduation, he became a certified forester and began selling timber. He married, expanded his business to include real estate and development, and began making money. And he continued to hunt.

In the spring of 1988 his life was changed in the second it takes to pull a trigger. "A friend and I were turkey hunting on a farm in Wilkes County," he began. "About midmorning we heard two gobblers gobbling at each other a few hundred yards away. We decided to split up and approach them from different directions. Big mistake. I followed a fence line for a couple of hundred yards and turned down a ditch that ran through a large hardwood drain toward the turkeys. I could hear them a short distance away over a ridge, so I crawled down the ditch until I found good cover. Then I yelped and they both gobbled. I got my gun up. Any second now I knew I would see those red and white heads popping over the ridge. But then I started to sense that something wasn't right. I don't know how, I could just tell it. I turned around and seen my hunting partner laying in the prone position about thirty-five yards behind me, aiming in the direction of the turkeys and me. I felt then that he knew I was there so I decided to try to call them on in, thinking we might both get shots.

"The turkeys came over the ridge before I was ready. I must have moved because they took off running. I raised up to shoot and immediately felt the most incredible impact you can ever imagine. It slammed me to the ground and when I raised up I realized that I was bleeding everywhere around my head. My ears were ringing and I was struggling to stay conscious. My hunting buddy was leaning over me and I could see this look of horror on his face. I jumped up and ran, just like a wounded animal. Ran out into a field and fell. My buddy caught up with me and started tearing my shirt off. I was on my hands and knees, and this puddle of blood on the ground under my head and chest, it just kept getting bigger and bigger. I was bleeding from my nose and my ears and my mouth.

"I begged my buddy to go get the truck, but he was afraid I wouldn't be alive when he got back. I told him the things I wanted him to tell Laura for me and that I forgave him for shooting me and not to let the accident ruin his life. He wanted to pray for me. I told him he could pray on his way to the truck, get going. After he left, I laid there trying to remain conscious, and then I started to pray myself. I didn't know who I was praying to, but whoever it was, I asked him to forgive me for my sins and to give me a chance to redeem myself. I guess I was asking Christ to come into my life, but what I wanted right then was for God to be with me. Whatever it was, He understood, and the fear began to subside. I felt the presence of peace so strong, it was like somebody laid a blanket over me. Like somebody was holding me. Whatever happened, I knew then that I'd be all right. It was not until I got to the emergency room that the pain started. I had more than thirty pellets of number four shot in my head and neck and back, had a severed nerve in my face and serious damage to my inner ear. It was just a miracle that I didn't lose an eye."

THE STORY of Steve's conversion did not explain his attitude toward hunting, but it resonated with love, which embraces and exceeds all codes of ethics. And though he spoke more freely and confidently of the mystery of the divine than I might have done, his words had the authority of a shotgun blast.

"You want to know the real reason I asked you to come on the safari?" he said.

"I sure do."

"Because God told me to. And I'll tell you something else, Doc. He had to keep telling me because I didn't want to ask you."

"Yeah, I was kinda surprised myself."

"But every time I prayed about it, your name was the only one that kept coming up. Then, when I saw you standing over there by yourself, at the retreat, God said, 'Okay, do it now. Go on and ask him. Right now.' But even then I was hoping that you'd say no. Then, the way you jumped at it, I figured you must have gotten the same message."

"Oh, I got the message all right."

III

A STATUE of David Livingstone stands upon a pedestal of rough-hewn granite on the banks of the Zambezi River near the great falls he named for Queen Victoria. Another occupies a niche in the outer wall of the Royal Geographical Society in London. Both locations are appropriate sites for a monument to the Scottish missionary doctor who trekked across south-central Africa when it was still a blank spot on the map. In both places he stands imperious and indefatigable, as befits a stone icon. The man himself was more complicated.

When I left for Africa, I knew little about him, only that he was a nineteenth-century medical missionary and explorer and that he was "found," or located, in the heart of Africa by Henry Morton Stanley, who greeted him with the famous phrase "Dr. Livingstone, I presume?" I knew also that he had searched for the source of the Nile, but I had never been particularly interested in him until I saw the movie *Mountains of the Moon,* which is based on the story of the explorer Richard Burton. Livingstone appears in only one scene, which, though fictitious, is true to the spirits of both men. Sequestered alone in a chamber of the Royal Geographical Society, they have just met for the first time. They eye each other warily, neither quite approving of the other. At last Livingstone asks Burton about a scar on his cheek. Burton says that he was struck in the face by a tribesman's spear. Livingstone exposes his scarred left shoulder and says, "Lion." In a superb demonstration of the competitiveness of male egos, the two middle-aged, formally dressed Victorian gentlemen proceed to remove clothing to reveal the wounds that authenticate their adventures. Burton shows a bullet hole. Livingstone drops his trousers, exposing a scar on his buttocks. "Scorpion," he says. Burton counters with calves scarred by lancing a disease of the legs, and Livingstone holds up a finger. "Rat," he explains. The scene is not history but it's marvelous Hollywood, and it prompted me to stuff into my carry-on bag a one-volume compilation of Livingstone's journals, which were published originally in three titles: *Missionary Travels and Researches in South Africa* (1857), *Narrative of an Expedition to the Zambesi and its Tributaries* (1865), and *The Last Journals of David Livingstone in Central Africa* (1874).

DAVID LIVINGSTONE was born in Blantyre, Scotland, in 1813, son of a poor tea salesman. The large family lived in a one-room tenement, subject not only to poverty but to the elder Livingstone's harsh religious dogma. When David and his two brothers reached the age of ten, they had to go to work at a cotton mill. In a culture in which most children grew up semiliterate at best, the boy found time to learn reading, arithmetic, and Latin. At nineteen he read a book that reconciled for him the apparent conflict between faith and science, for which he had an aptitude, and at the same time provided an alternative to the Calvinist doctrine of the elect. "I saw the duty and inestimable privilege immediately to accept salvation by Christ," he wrote. By the age of twenty-three he had saved enough money to leave the mill and enroll in medical studies. Though none of his instructors found him brilliant, they were impressed by his determination and self-discipline. Years later he would write, "In the glow of love which Christianity inspires I soon resolved to devote my life to the alleviation of human misery." The dour young Scot decided on China as a mission field, but the outbreak of the Opium Wars combined with the influence of Robert Moffat, missionary to South Africa, changed his mind. In 1841, at the age of twenty-eight, he arrived at Moffat's station in Kuruman, where he discovered to his dismay that Moffat and other missionaries had had little success in converting native people. Establishing his own station at Mabotsa, 250 miles northeast of Kuruman, he determined to do better.

Livingstone's legacy remains to this day a matter of dispute. He achieved great fame in his lifetime. His funeral at Westminster Abbey was the largest since that of Wellington. Twenty-five years later many of his countrymen considered him the greatest Englishman of the Victorian period. Nor was his acclaim limited to Britain. Among Africans he was known as "the friend of Africans," and the cities of Livingstone, Zambia, and Blantyre, Malawi, are among the few colonial place names in central Africa that were retained by the independent governments.

But what was he famous for? The answer depends on who you ask. His biographer Tim Jeal says that he converted only one African to Christianity and that one soon lapsed. The single British stamp on which he appears is part of a set honoring great explorers, but Livingstone himself insisted repeatedly that he was always a missionary first and an explorer almost by default. As he wrote in a now-famous statement at the end of his first book, *Missionary Travels and Researches*, "I view the end of the geographical feat as the beginning of the missionary enterprise," by which he meant that the slave trade had to be abolished and the country opened to industry, agriculture, and commerce before Christianity could take root. His task was to blaze the trail that less intrepid souls might follow.

Politically correct opinion of our time condemns Livingstone as an apostle of "commerce and Christianity," the very role for which he was celebrated a century ago. Not only that, scholars have found texts to prove that he was humorless, irascible, vindictive, intolerant of other missionaries, insensitive to his long-suffering wife and children, and even occasionally profane, so how could he be a saint? And they like to dwell on the conflict between his religious faith and his allegedly self-serving determination to establish an English colony on the Shire River and to discover the source of the Nile. Livingstone struggled with those conflicts, to be sure, but I believe that the true dynamic of his complex nature was the tension between his devout love of the Creator and his impassioned devotion to the creation, especially in Africa.

Because Livingstone's books were written for public consumption, they may not be the most reliable record of his faith, but his private letters confirm the report of his journals: he had a passion for God that did not falter; he was a man of prayer and a faithful reader of the Bible. It was because of his sense of Christ's love, he said, that he loved others and apparently believed that he had been anointed, or at least commissioned, to heal the sick and to set the captives free, not only from sin but first and above all from the devastating effects of the slave trade.

But Livingstone also loved Africa. Its sights, sounds, and smells, its seasons and its weather—its colors—had gotten into his metaphysical blood as surely as malaria parasites infected his liver, and he could never eradicate it. After trekking across half of the south end of the continent and arriving almost dead of fever at the coast of Portuguese West Africa, he firmly resisted attempts by British naval officers to take him back to England. He had not seen his wife and young children in three years, but he was determined to turn around and march east to the Indian Ocean, a journey that would take another three. When he returned home at last, he remained for only eighteen months.

His next expedition, the Zambezi, was a disaster in almost every way, not the least of which was the death of Livingstone's wife, Mary, from fever. Devastated by grief, he buried her on the banks of the river and pressed on, determined still to open a path for colonization. But his efforts resulted indirectly in the deaths of several missionaries and the failure of the mission they sought to establish. He returned home discredited. He was fifty-one years old, his health was impaired by years of hardship, and he had never even laid eyes on his youngest child, Anna Mary. It made no sense to his family that he should want to return to Africa, but to his brother Charles he wrote, "I don't know whether I am to go on the shelf or not. If I do, I make Africa the shelf." Back in Africa for the last time, determined now to discover the source of the Nile, he wrote, "The mere animal pleasure of travelling in a wild unexplored country is very great."

LIVINGSTONE was attacked during his own lifetime and has been ever since as a missionary more interested in his own glory than

God's and as an explorer who half the time had no idea where he was. There is no point in trying to counter those charges. What is undeniable is that Livingstone loved God and he loved Africa. As I discovered the passions that governed him, he assumed a major presence in my anticipation of the trip.

Part Two

AN OBSERVER'S JOURNAL

... though I had no wish to shoot a big animal myself, hunting dangerous game is a part of the African mystique that I did not know. And this morning is a soft green morning when death, which never seems remote in Africa, but hangs about like something half-remembered, might come almost companionably . . .

PETER MATTHIESSEN, *The Tree Where Man Was Born*

I am certain that the hunt is part of the hardwiring of humanity.

JOHN HEMINWAY, *No Man's Land*

IV

▼▼▼▼▼

BY THE TIME WE landed in Johannesburg, my sense of the time of day had been obliterated by the intercontinental flight. Through the large windows of the terminal I could see that it was light outside but whether morning or afternoon I couldn't tell without looking at my watch. After a brief layover, we boarded another 747 for Lusaka, the capital of Zambia. An hour or so later I stepped from the plane onto the platform of mobile stairs and felt the bright breeze blowing across the tarmac. This light was different from any I had ever seen. I looked toward the blue hills in the distance and breathed it in.

From the platform, there was nothing particularly African about the shiny modern airport. We climbed aboard a bus and rode across the runway. Inside the building we followed the crowd that went through the "International Visitors" door to "Passports and Visas." Stamped and certified, we headed for baggage claim, uncertain what to do beyond that point.

DURING Steve Ebbert's earlier trip to South Africa a man had told him that rural Africans were in desperate need of footwear. "Shoes are as good as gold over here," the man had said, "especially tennis shoes. When you come back, you need to bring shoes. You can trade them for anything." Soon after inviting me to go with him to Zambia, Steve had explained the shoe project. But instead of taking shoes for barter, he said, he planned to give them away. "To whom?" I asked.

"To the tribe that lives in the area where we'll be hunting. We'll take as many as we can carry."

Word of the project got out, and Steve was interviewed by a local paper. I cringed when I saw the headline: "Hunter Has Shoe Mission During African Safari." No telling what Steve had said to the reporter or what she would make of his comments.

> Although he is an avid hunter, it is the shoes—not the game—that Ebbert said he's most excited about.
>
> "This means a lot to me. It means every bit as much to me as the safari," he said. "What we want to do is really encourage others, who might be traveling to Third World countries or poverty-stricken areas or even in this country, to find a need in that area that they can satisfy with their time, talents, and money."
>
> Ebbert said he was reluctant to discuss the details of the trip and the mission work publicly because he didn't want to give the wrong impression about why he was doing it.
>
> "If this encourages others to do this then we have done the right thing. But if it makes one person feel like we're glamorizing what we're doing or raising ourselves up, then we've done a terrible thing," Ebbert said.
>
> "What I want to demonstrate is Christianity through action—not just through telling people I'm a Christian," he added.
>
> Ebbert has . . . asked two other Athens residents to accompany him . . . Jim Kilgo, a novelist and retired English professor . . . and Stuart McLean, a UGA journalism student.

I winced at the sight of my name. If the reporter was going to represent me as a missionary, even by association, she might at least have called me for my side of the story. But even if she had, I didn't know what I would have said. In telling people that I was going to Africa, I had spoken not only of a geographical location but of a timeless ideal as well, the big game safari that I had read about from childhood in books by Roosevelt, Dinesen, Hemingway, Hunter, and Ruark. Though I was aware of the contemporary African world of poverty and AIDS and genocide, I had not allowed it to impinge on my dream. Somehow, I had supposed, we would be transported into the center of the Upper Lupande Game Management Area, where we would settle in with drinks beside a campfire and listen to the sounds of the African night and talk about hunting. But this shoe business was a reminder that the safari would occur in a cultural context. People lived in the bush, in small villages around the boundary of the GMA. Many of them were sick; all were poor, hungry, and barefooted. Steve said that putting shoes on their feet was the least we could do.

I didn't know. Christians are asked to clothe the naked, but I was not convinced that bare feet in central Africa was what Jesus meant by naked. How cold did it get in Zambia? Besides, shoes don't last forever. Was it really charitable to create a need that we could not continue to supply? Nike cross-trainers in a village of people whose feet were hardened to the bush seemed absurd to me, especially when offered in the name of Jesus. But this was Steve's show, I reminded myself. I was going as an observer, by his good pleasure. The least I could do was shoulder my share of the shoes and keep my mouth shut.

So I joined Steve and Stuart one hot afternoon to pack eight large duffel bags. But when Steve announced that we were going to take a thousand little pocket crosses too, I balked. We could hand them out with the shoes, he said.

"Y'all can," I said, "but don't you think it might be better to wait and see if people want them?"

WHEN THE LUGGAGE you checked at the point of departure appears out of that mysterious mouth at the head of the carousel in the airport of your destination, it seems miraculous, even more so when you have crossed the Atlantic. We had checked fifteen bags in Atlanta, and here they came, onto the conveyor belt in Lusaka, our burden once again. We started grabbing—the bulky black canvas duffels containing shoes, four, five, six, seven, eight, and the four grossly overweight green bags, stuffed with personal gear and boxes of Steve's arrows. All these we heaved from the conveyor belt to the floor. But where were the metal cases, the carefully packed rifles and bows? Steve had brought three, but none came down the carousel.

"I'll probably have to pick them up at another place," Steve said. "I'll meet you at customs."

Stuart had found carts. We began stacking bags.

A WELL-DRESSED young woman at customs welcomed us to her country with a bored, officious smile. What's in the bags, she wanted to know, drumming her fingers. English is the official language of Zambia, legacy of the British colonial government, and the clerk spoke it the way she had learned it in school, with self-conscious precision.

Her question was answered by a large, handsome woman who had suddenly appeared in our midst. Steve introduced her to Stuart and me as Beatrice, assistant to the owner of the safari company, a man named Ahmad. Beatrice had come to pick us up, assist us through customs, and take us to a hotel in town, for we had arrived too late to catch the single daily flight to Mfuwe, which was our final destination. Beatrice was smartly dressed; her copper-tinted hair, tightly woven into a thousand tiny braids and bound into a sheaf, hung on her neck like a metallic mane. She was accompanied by a tall, pretty young woman who smiled shyly when I asked her to repeat her name—Kangwa.

Beatrice explained to the clerk in a language they shared—probably Bemba—that the bags contained shoes.

For whom?

Steve stepped forward and spoke to the clerk in the loud voice that is natural to him. "We brought these shoes to give to the people who live in the area where we're going to be hunting."

She all but rolled her eyes. "What is the value?"

Steve looked at me and shrugged. Whether this was licensed extortion, bureaucratic zeal, or merely animosity toward Americans, neither of us could tell. Unable to assess the value of the shoes, Steve laughed and said, "Ten dollars a bag," though he had spent eight hundred dollars of his own money in shipping costs.

The clerk was not amused. How much did we pay for them, she wanted to know.

"We didn't pay anything for them. They were donated by churches in Athens, Georgia, where we live."

"Open the bags," she said.

"All of them?"

"All of them."

The demand was outrageous—the bags contained hundreds of pairs of shoes and we were obviously safari clients, not black market operators—but I was reminded that David Livingstone had had to bribe his way through many of the territories he traveled. Such extortion, I supposed, must be an ancient practice among African gatekeepers.

Steve leaned across the counter, supporting himself by his short arms. "Listen," he said. "If you insist on making this difficult, people in my country are going to stop sending things to help your people."

Steve spoke calmly, but I winced. Such a threat was not going to faze this young woman. You could see how much she cared about the words "your people."

"Open the bags."

"I want to talk with your supervisor," Steve said.

The clerk turned and spoke to an older, even more officious woman who had been following the discussion from her glass cubicle a few feet away. As she approached, Beatrice spoke to her, again in Bemba. The customs official folded her arms across her chest, pulled down the window shades of her face, and hung out a sign that said "closed." Steve raised his eyebrows, shrugged, and heaved a bag onto the counter.

As though that were the signal for which he'd been waiting, a man stepped forward. His dark beard was flecked with gray, and his open collar revealed a hairy throat. He looked Indian. With a jerk of his head he directed the official back to her cubicle, leaned in at the window, and spoke quietly. She replied. He took a bill from his wallet and handed it to her then came over to Steve. The entire transaction had taken less than thirty seconds.

"Okay," Steve said to us, "let's get this stuff out of here before they change their mind."

"Was that Ahmad?" I asked.

"That's exactly who it was."

"What did he say to her?"

"I don't know, but it cost me a hundred bucks."

"Think what it would have cost if he hadn't been here."

Steve seemed distracted, but in a second he snapped out of his daze. "That's exactly right," he said.

STEVE HAD BOOKED this trip through an outdoors adventure agency in Chattanooga. The agent worked with a Zambian professional hunter named Harry Chapman, whom Steve had requested. Harry was employed by Sable Safaris, owned by Ahmad, who held the lease on the Luangwa River concession where we would be hunting. This was a standard arrangement, but having to deal with three parties made it hard to know which was in charge, which man answerable to the client. At the moment Steve's chief concern was the whereabouts of his bows and rifles. Ahmad had departed with a couple of German clients, leaving us to the care of Beatrice.

From the office of Zambia Air, Steve and Beatrice placed calls to South Africa Air in Johannesburg, Delta in Atlanta, and the agent in Chattanooga. After an hour of international tracking, Steve concluded that no one had the slightest idea what had become of the missing cases, but South Africa Air assured Steve that they would be in Lusaka before our departure the next day for Mfuwe.

By the time we were ready to leave the airport Ahmad had returned. It would take two vehicles to transport us and our mountain of gear into town. I rode with Ahmad in his pickup. We passed without trouble through a checkpoint manned by soldiers and turned onto the highway toward the city. On the right stood a billboard depicting a map of the country, bright red against the rest of the continent, and a caption proclaiming that Zambia is "the real Africa."

BEFORE ZAMBIA became Zambia, it was Northern Rhodesia, but before that, the territory was a vast terra incognita that spread across the Central African Plateau, dotted by small villages of Bantu tribes who lived by hunting, fishing, and subsistence agriculture. After the seventeenth century, Arab and Portuguese slave traders made occasional forays north of the Zambezi River, but the area was unknown to European exploration—specifically, to Britain's Royal Geographic Society—until the arrival of David Livingstone, who "discovered" the Zambezi in 1851. When the European powers sat down in 1884, ten years after Livingstone's death, to carve up Africa, Britain, largely on the basis of the missionary activity stimulated by Livingstone, claimed most of the land between the southern border of Congo Free State, which belonged to King Leopold II of Belgium, and the Limpopo River, now the border between Zimbabwe and South Africa. Five years later, Britain granted a young English entrepreneur named Cecil Rhodes a charter that empowered his company, the British South Africa Company, to stake claims in the area. Leopold's insistence on retaining a section of rich copper deposits resulted in the peculiar shape of modern Zambia. To my eye it resembles two rough circles of unequal size joined at the bottom by a narrow strip of land.

From 1924 to 1964 Northern Rhodesia was a British protectorate interested chiefly in profits from the country's copper mines. Independence fever began to spread among the black population in the fifties. In 1964 the United National Independence Party, led by Kenneth Kaunda, won control of the legislative council, and by the end of the year it had peacefully negotiated the country's independence from Britain. The new country took its name from the Zambezi River, which separated it from Southern Rhodesia. In an uncontested election Kaunda became president, a position he held for thirty years. Although his Marxist government was often charged with corruption, Kaunda maintained a degree of political stability in Zambia during a period when surrounding states were tearing themselves apart by civil war. In 1991, confident of his power, he acceded to the demands of other parties for open elections. To his surprise, he was soundly defeated by Frederick Chiluba of the Movement for Multiparty Democracy. When we arrived in Zambia, Chiluba was in the last year of his second and final term.

As Ahmad drove me into Lusaka, he told me that Kaunda had almost destroyed the country but Chiluba had come along just in time. Because of his reforms, things had been getting better ever since. I asked him if the extortion at the airport was a holdover from the old administration, but he just shrugged in that universal gesture that can mean either yes or no. Though our difficulties at customs seemed outrageous to me, Ahmad apparently considered it merely the cost of doing business.

Driving through outlying slums of Lusaka, we passed a large flock of guinea fowl pecking about on the grassy shoulder of the road. I asked Ahmad if they were wild birds. He said they were—helmeted guinea fowl, my first African species.

The ten-mile stretch between the airport and Lusaka reminded me of approaches to Third World cities I had seen in Brazil and Costa Rica. The four-lane highway, cratered with potholes, runs straight across flat, scrubby country. Foot and bicycle traffic were heavy in the dusty paths alongside the pavement. Women wrapped in bright prints balanced weighty burdens on their heads—bundles of long sugar cane, baskets of clothing, sometimes a cage of chickens. Many also carried infants slung on their backs or nursing at their breasts. Old men and boys maneuvered unbalanced, front-laden bicycles along the same paths, recklessly close to whizzing trucks and mini-vans, and shirtless young men were gathered on corners smoking cigarettes and laughing. Scrubby brush half concealed the tin-roofed shacks where these people lived.

Lusaka has a population of two million, twenty percent of Zambia's ten million, with more arriving from rural villages every day, seeking jobs that don't exist. A billboard depicting beggars and cripples announced COMMUNITY BASED REHABILITATION IS THE ANSWER. DO NOT GIVE ALMS TO STREET BEGGARS. And on the side of a building a nicely painted mural showing a Zambian doctor talking with two or three young people simply proclaimed ANTI-AIDS PROJECT.

Suddenly we had entered an area of housing projects, schools, and shopping centers. Billboards advertised Blockbusters, the Gap, and local banks. We passed the gate to the University of Zambia on the left. At a major intersection spanned by a shining red footbridge, Ahmad guided the pickup through highway construction and turned into a wide boulevard shaded by trees that looked like mimosas. Before us rose the tall, glittering buildings of downtown Lusaka—the city's surprising skyline. Whether or not this sociological brew of poverty, disease, and prosperity was what the sign meant by "the real Africa," it was for me only an unavoidable portal to the old Africa I was seeking.

Ahmad followed Beatrice into the parking lot of a Holiday Inn. Twenty minutes later, each of us settled in his air-conditioned room, I might as well have been back in Atlanta.

▼ ▼ ▼

ON THE WAY to the airport the next morning, I asked Kangwa if she had ever visited Harry Chapman's Upper Lupande camp. She made a face as though I had asked the most ridiculous question she had ever heard. "I hate the bush," she said. "All those lions and snakes. No thank you."

We left for Mfuwe without the arms cases. Rumor had it that they had made it as far as Harare and would surely arrive in Lusaka in time for the next day's flight, but they didn't. Ahmad promised to send them on, but Steve would now miss at least one expensive day of hunting.

From the air, slums and shantytowns spread from the city like a vast scabby rash on the skin of the countryside. By the time we had gained our altitude, though, slums gave way to bush, *miombo* woodland flat and open, dotted with small villages. We flew northeast. The wing of the twin-engine reflected the blinding sun, and far below, the shadow of the plane skimmed along a flashing river. I took it to be the Luangwa. June in the southern hemisphere is the beginning of winter, which is the dry season in equatorial Africa. By now most of the streams were sandy beds, but the Luangwa, which runs southwest to join the great Zambezi, flows throughout the year, and that perennial supply of water would concentrate animals in the riverine forest.

On the western side of the valley stood the steep wall of the Muchinga Escarpment, but the eastern side rose gradually in a series of low hills and ridges. In some places along its length the Luangwa Valley is sixty miles wide. Geologists have suggested that it is a small finger of the Great Rift that splits the crust of the continent from the Red Sea to Mozambique. At the upper end of the valley, near the border of Tanzania, archeologists have discovered evidence of the earliest use of fire by homo sapiens, but the landscape below showed no sign of human activity, not a settlement, not a path. I was reminded of Isak Dinesen's description of the Kenya highlands in *Out of Africa*: "There was no fat on it and no luxuriance anywhere. . . . The colours were dry and burnt, like the colours in pottery."

There were few passengers on the small commuter—two or three native Africans, a group of five men and women whose accents sounded British, and a young couple from America, who, as Steve learned, had worked together in the Peace Corps and were returning to Mfuwe to get married. The British were sitting behind me. The noise of the engines drowned out their conversation, but I caught the word "safari" several times. I thought for a moment of asking them where they were going, but then I would have had to explain what we were doing in the Luangwa Valley, and something told me that they would not have welcomed the information.

HARRY CHAPMAN stood in the doorway of the small Mfuwe airport, waiting to greet us. I had seen a video of one of his safaris so I recognized him right away. He was a tall man, a light-skinned Zambian of mixed blood, whose stance, expression, and demeanor declared plainly that he knew his business. The authority in his face suggested a man of about forty, though in fact, as I was to learn, he was only thirty-two. Steve had met him in January at the Safari Club International convention in Reno, and they greeted each other now with the warmth of old friends. "This is Stuart," Steve said, "and this is Doc." Harry introduced two of his people, a blond South African named Jason and a dark-skinned young man called Karim who looked as Arabic as his name sounded. Both were apprentice PH's. Jason, though young, exemplified the prototype of the profession, and his accent caused the atmosphere to feel more African. Karim, who was Harry's cousin, was strikingly handsome, and his perfect white teeth flashed when he smiled.

A life-sized mahogany giraffe stood at one end of the narrow lobby, a stalking lion at the other. On one of the walls, schoolchildren had painted a mural of local animals—zebras, buffalo, giraffe, lions, and leopards—but the bold primary colors indicated that the little artists had had no more personal experience of the creatures than Kangwa had. The caption—ENJOY OUR ANIMALS—reminded me that the animals of the Luangwa Valley were commodities, whether for sale to hunters like Steve or to tourists like the group of British, who were eyeing us with disapproval as Harry's men loaded our luggage onto handcarts. Though there were no weapons cases among our gear, the tourists seemed somehow to know that Harry and his men were a hunting operation.

In parking spaces outside stood a row of Toyota Land Cruisers, apparently the vehicle of choice among safari operators, for each of these displayed upon its door panels the logos of lodges and safari companies—Kapani, Robin Pope, and our own Sable Safaris. Harry's two vehicles were soon piled high with luggage and men— the three of us, the three professional hunters, and several local staff people, who in the early days of African safaris would have worked as porters, carrying our gear on their heads. I wondered how far we had to go to reach the bush. Our little caravan was soon speeding down a straight paved road, built, Harry explained, by former President Kaunda to facilitate travel from the airport to his private lodge in the South Luangwa National Park. "Enjoy it while it lasts," Jason said. "We won't be on it long."

I looked about for a town that might be large enough to host an airport, but all I could see of Mfuwe were houses along the highway, brick or block bungalows, some with thatch roofs, half-hidden among banana fronds, millet patches, and shade trees, or round grass huts standing in the middle of bare, swept yards. Except for the grass construction of huts and cribs, the scene reminded me of the rural

South in the 1940s. Like the highway into Lusaka, this road was bordered on both sides by hard-packed paths that bore witness to heavy bicycle and pedestrian traffic. These women too were heavily laden with bundles on their heads and infants on their backs, these men shirtless, smiling, and unhurried. Children of all ages, some in school uniforms, some in rags, pursued their serious little purposes up and down the road, headed who knew where. The younger ones smiled and waved, but teenagers of both sexes were too cool even to notice the safari vehicles carrying white foreigners out into the bush.

We turned off the pavement onto a dirt road. The second vehicle, bearing the staff and most of our luggage, hung back to allow our dust to settle. We passed a school and a small settlement, then infrequent clearings with round grass huts and scrubby garden plots. Except for a few scrawny, head-pecked chickens I saw no livestock, neither goats nor cattle. The reason for that, I had read, is the tsetse fly—in the Luangwa Valley, *Glossina morsitansis*—vector for the blood parasite *Trypanosoma,* which causes sleeping sickness in both humans and domestic stock but not in wild animals.

Through occasional clearings in the brush, the still-green country rolled gently toward the blue swells of the eastern hills.

The road narrowed to a single track, the woods closed in on both sides, and suddenly birds were everywhere. "We are entering the bush now," Karim said. He spoke so softly I barely understood him. He was sitting with Stuart and me on the high bench behind the front bucket seats where Steve was riding. Jason stood in the rear, leaning against the back of the bench, close enough for conversation. It didn't take long to discover that he knew birds. For the rest of the way I pointed and he called out names. The most abundant species along the road was a small, boldly patterned, brown and white finchlike bird that was constantly flying up before the vehicle: white-browed sparrow weaver, Jason said. A grackle-sized bird that flashed a gloriously intense blue in its wings as it flew he identified as a lilac-breasted roller. Once a small black bird with a long train of a tail beat its way with difficulty up into a tree in front of us. When it alighted on a branch I could see gold on the back of its neck and russet on its throat.

Paradise whydah, Jason said. Doves of several species flushed before us all the way, and hawks, too swift in flight for Jason to recognize, swooped across openings in the canopy. How far into the bush we would have to go before animals appeared, I did not know. It was hard to imagine such creatures as buffalo and elephants standing like deer just inside the trees, but the track was littered with fresh droppings of large beasts.

A hundred yards up ahead six or eight light-colored baboons loped across the track and disappeared into cover. Karim said they were yellow baboons, the only species of that primate that occurs in the valley. As I searched the woods on the right where they had gone, a flock of large birds appeared—as big as turkeys but bulky and black with long heavy bills and conspicuous red wattling around the eyes and red pouches on their throats. Ground hornbills. I would learn later from our trackers that the species is treated by native tribesmen as special, if not sacred: they are never hunted, and to see them at the beginning of a hunt is considered a sign of good luck, especially if they are moving in the opposite direction as these were.

After ten miles or so we turned onto a rougher, narrower track. Harry slowed down, but even so the three of us on the high bench seat had to stay alert for overhanging branches. When we crossed dry streambeds, Harry would come almost to a full stop and look up and down the twisting sandy course. I was beginning to believe in the possibility of animals, but all we saw were small, rufus-colored squirrels scurrying from one side of the road to the other, right under the tires of the vehicle.

Except for dips into streambeds, the valley floor was flat, but the vegetation was changing constantly from open mopani woodland to thickets of *Combretum ovobatum* and acacia to stands of long grass that we had to brush aside as we passed, then back to thicket again. Ahead, low over the track, loomed the thick limb of a large tree— perhaps a ficus—a perfect-looking spot for a picture-book leopard.

And then Karim said, "Here we are."

Before us stood a grove of trees surrounded by a wall of thatched grass and in the wall a roofed gateway. "Watch your head," Karim warned. We ducked as we drove through the portal. On the left, in a line, stood ten or twelve men in white clothes, clapping and chanting, broad smiles in their dark faces.

Harry stepped down from behind the wheel. "Welcome to the camp," he said. "This is home for the next three weeks."

Home. But for only three weeks. It felt like a place I could stay for the rest of my life. The camp lay in the shelter of a grove of tall trees—sausage trees, ebonies, Natal mahoganies, and figs—a half-acre of hard-packed gray dirt, as flat as a tennis court and scored by the shallow grooves of rakes. Not a leaf in sight. The grass fence surrounding the compound and separating us from the bush stood eight feet high on the back side but only three on the front, affording a wide, unobstructed view of the sunny Luangwa River two hundred yards out.

Harry had parked the Land Cruiser alongside a grass and pole building with a cement floor, open sides, and a peaked roof. "This is the dining hut," he said. It faced the river. At the other end of the compound stood three chalets of the same grass and pole construction, set on slabs. One entered through a little stoop into a comfortable, airy room with two beds and bamboo shelves. An en suite stall for shower and toilet completed the accommodations. The chalet at the far end was Harry's, the other two ours. Steve suggested that Stuart and I might be more comfortable bunking together because of his prodigious snoring.

The camp was a congenial space. After unpacking and stowing my gear, I slung binoculars around my neck and walked out under the trees. Beyond the cool island of the grove the afternoon was warm and bright. The air was filled with calls of unfamiliar birds, the most dominant of which was a guttural three-syllable phrase that to my ear sounded like pon-*tal*-ba, pon-*tal*-ba, endlessly repeated—the Cape turtle dove. For the next three weeks we would never find ourselves beyond the range of its tireless voice.

A small patio abutted the front of the compound, a sort of open-air veranda with chairs arranged around a fire pit in the center of its cement floor—the after-dark storytelling place, I figured. An opening in the low wall permitted access to a path that took one down a grassy bank and out onto the wide, sandy river beach. During the rainy season, from November to May, the Luangwa would escape its banks, filling the flood plain with a racing muddy current that would eat at the banks and overflow the higher ground beneath the grove. Roads would become waterways, impossible to negotiate in a vehicle, and if the rains were heavy the entire valley would be inundated. This year the rains had continued into May, much later than usual. The long grass, normally brown by now, was still rank, too green to burn, but the river had returned to its winding dry-season channel. Though still broad and muddy, it flowed at a leisurely rate. Above the river dozens of slender crimson birds were hawking for insects, swooping and darting in the burning air. I was having trouble catching and holding them in the binoculars.

"Carmine bee-eaters," said Jason, who had joined me on the beach. "They nest in the river banks." He pronounced the name cahr-*mine,* which in his South African accent I failed for a moment to understand, but, familiar with the name and the species from my field guide, I quickly figured out what he had said and was delighted to discover the gorgeous birds in our own front yard.

"Did you notice the hippos, Doc?"

"Hippos?"

"Over along the far bank."

Two of them, he said, but I had to take his word for it; even through binoculars I could see nothing more than bumps breaking the surface of the water. Jason had good eyes.

"I think lunch is ready," he said.

I had forgotten I was hungry, though it was almost four o'clock.

A YOUNG WOMAN was sitting at the table in the dining hut. Harry introduced her as his wife, Layla. Her large, dark eyes flickered for an instant on my face as she smiled and offered her hand. She had spent time in front of a mirror arranging her long hair and applying makeup, but she was as shy as she was lovely. She looked down at her lap again in self-conscious silence. Or maybe the self-consciousness was all my own, projected onto her.

When we were served, Steve asked me to say a blessing. An awkward request. Was he the host, or were we guests of the Muslim PH? He and Harry were seated at opposite ends of the table but which end was considered the head? None of us knew the proprieties, but clearly Steve was assuming the right. I had no desire to offend, but my delight in Africa, my joy in the opportunity after so many years to be in this very place, hearing bird calls that I had never heard before, spilled over in spontaneous praise of the Creator we all acknowledged.

No sooner had I said "Amen" when Harry said "Elephants."

There were two, on the opposite bank four hundred yards away, proceeding downstream like lords of the valley to whom the concerns of lesser creatures like ourselves were trivial. I grabbed my binoculars, silenced by my first sight of these creatures in the wild, these incarnations of Africa—even at such a distance huge, ponderous, and improbable. Now was the time to give thanks.

"Bulls?" Steve asked.

"Yes," Harry said.

"Are they good ones?"

"Aaah, sixty pounds maybe. Not bad."

Harry was estimating the weight of the tusks. There had been a time when it would have taken a hundred-pounder to be considered "not bad," but that was before ivory poaching in the 1970s and '80s reduced the Luangwa herd from one hundred thousand to a meager five thousand. I had read the story in *The Eye of the Elephant* by Mark and Delia Owens, or as much of it as had developed by the time they wrote the book in 1991.

As THE SERVANTS cleared the table, Harry said, "Let's go for a ride."

We climbed back into the Land Cruiser, claiming the seats we had occupied on the way to camp. A tracker named Demetrius joined Jason in the rear.

With camera and binoculars around my neck and a monopod at my feet, I felt encumbered, but the optics, provided by Steve, were my assigned way of seeing the country, the apparatus of an observer. Outside the gate, just beyond a marula tree, Harry turned left onto a narrow, bumpy track crowded on both sides with long grass, higher than our heads, and headed north, upriver. We lurched along slowly, screened by the dense growth on either side. Harry rounded a bend and stopped. On our right, not more than twenty steps away, stood an elephant, all dusty, baggy skin and polished tusks. The grass was trampled flat in a wide circle around him. I fumbled for the camera. His massive head swung toward us, trunk uplifted, searching for our scent. I zoomed in on his eye, bright reddish brown and webbed all around with the wrinkles of great age. There had been no time to attach the monopod, which would have been useless anyway because of the vibrations of the running engine. Why doesn't Harry switch it off? I wondered, and immediately I had my answer. The elephant spread its ears, raised its trunk, and surged toward us. Harry dropped the shifter into low, and the vehicle leaped, nearly upending Jason and Demetrius in back. Then the elephant trumpeted, a sound as big and as serious as the creature who made it. I felt thoroughly dismissed. Jason and Demetrius laughed. Harry smiled. "Young bull," he said, "feeling macho."

We soon passed a lagoon on the left, an oxbow long since cut off by the constantly changing meander of the river. Though the dry season was underway, the lagoon was full from the late rains. Lily pads covered the surface, and the banks were bright green with mats of aquatic vegetation. Through the great trees that surrounded it, hundreds of flushing ducks and geese hammered the air as they beat toward the sky. Harry slowed up. "White-faced ducks and Egyptian geese mostly," he said. I yearned to hop out and stay right there, perched on the bank, until dark, but Harry had already told us that we were never to leave the compound unaccompanied by an armed escort. "My father taught me two things," he said. "One, never trust the bush, and two, never trust the night." I was willing to take his word for it, but the bird-watcher in me groaned in frustration as we left the lagoon behind.

A flock of guinea fowl emerged from the grass on the right and scurried up the road before us, plump and blue, running fast, some of them darting back into cover. "Supper," Harry said and pulled to a stop. Karim took a shotgun from its case and handed it down to Steve, who was already on the ground and ready. In five fast steps he overtook the covey and flushed them; the semiautomatic spoke twice and three birds fell, one merely winged. Before the last of them hit the ground, Jason and Demetrius were tearing into the brush. Jason picked up two, and Demetrius ran down the cripple. Only then did I notice that he was barefooted.

"We were getting tired of canned chicken," Harry said. "We'll have those tonight and get real meat tomorrow."

Jason handed one of the birds to me. From a distance the helmeted guinea fowl looks just like the domestic guineas on farms in Georgia, but in my hand I could see a difference. Though speckled like our barnyard guinea, the native bird has a bright blue face and neck, a red cap, and a horny casque on its head. Its plump breast was still warm.

A mile or two further and the shrubby brush opened on the left upon the sandy bed of the Kauluzi, which flows into the Luangwa when it flows at all. A herd of puku—an antelope the size of a white-tailed deer—fed peacefully in the short grass of the wide green flood plain, unconcerned with lions. Their coats in the setting sun were burnished red-gold. They were beyond the reach of my extended lens, but through binoculars I brought them in close enough to inspect the horns on the males—not as long as an impala's but thicker and ringed with ridges, bending backward and out to form the shape of a shallow lyre.

As the sun went down you could begin to smell the bush: a rich brew of vegetation and animal musk, constantly shifting in the breeze. Once we drove into an effluvium that reeked so strongly of cat piss that I thought a lion or a leopard must have just sprayed the grass along the road. But Karim said no, it was a particular kind of mint, very common. "Cats have an odor of rotten meat," he said. I asked him if he could smell animals.

"Yes," he said. "Sometimes. Especially buffalo, zebra, elephant, and kudu."

My nose twitched.

A file of yellow-billed storks flew toward the west, into the reddening sky.

Before we got back to camp we spotted several herds of impala, zebras standing steady by the track in the dusk, trotting warthogs with their aerial tails, and at a distance a family group of elephants, but the only time Harry stopped was when Karim said "Kudu."

It was almost dark, but the word brought me to attention. Kudu was the antelope of the great spiraled horns, together with the sable the most prized of African plains game. By writing *Green Hills of Africa* about his hunt for these two elusive animals, Hemingway had endowed each species with a romantic aura of Old Africa. Eager to see in the flesh what had got him so excited, I leaned forward, straining my eyes for any flicker of movement in the thickety savanna. I thought I saw two large forms moving through shadows. "Females," Karim said.

I reached into my day pack for my hooded jacket. With the going down of the sun, the evening had grown surprisingly cool, and when Harry stepped on the gas, the wind in my face was chilling. All the way back, eyes of small creatures—close-set little coals—glowed up at us from the dusty road. Tiny hyraxes scampered back and forth as bush squirrels had during the day, and ghostly white birds fluttered up like moths in the beams of the headlights.

For many Americans the word "safari" evokes a Hollywood image of white hunter, rich but inept client, and pretty girlfriend, decked out in khaki shorts and pith helmets, leading a long line of native porters across an open plain teeming with herds of wildebeest, gazelle, zebra, and buffalo. This stereotype of East Africa may have originated in Rider Haggard's character Alan Quartermain, created on the model of Frederick Courtney Selous, but it was the Kenya safari of Teddy Roosevelt in 1909 that popularized big game hunting in Africa. As Americans and Europeans poured into Nairobi, white hunters like J. A. Hunter, Bror Blixen, and Philip Percival became legendary. The fraternity soon developed a camp protocol and a code of ethics, both of which are well represented in Hemingway's short story "The Short Happy Life of Francis Macomber." Since those fabled days, the center of safari hunting has shifted from Kenya, which banned hunting in 1977, to the south-central African states; "white hunters," not all of whom are white now, go by the inclusive name "professional hunter"; and life in the bush provides more amenities. Yet the code and the protocol remain fundamentally unchanged. As we rolled into camp after our drive through the bush, looking forward to a drink and a cigar by the fire, I found it easy to pretend that I was entering the world of Hemingway's story.

THE CAMPFIRE was made of mopani wood and gave off a distinctive, pungent smoke unlike any I had ever smelled at home. I pulled a chair up close, reached down into the fire pit for a burning stick, and lit a cigar. One bright star shone in the lingering, violet afterglow out over the river. Maybe it was one of the familiar planets from the Northern Hemisphere merely unrecognizable in this new place, or perhaps it was as strange as the exotic creatures we had seen that day.

The soft voice of one of the servants, who became visible in the shadows only by his white clothing, asked if I would like something to drink. My choices were limited to nonalcoholic. Whatever beer, wine, and whiskey Harry may have ordered had not yet arrived, but the air along the river was chilly enough for coffee. I asked the servant his name. In a whisper he said, "Bernard," pronouncing it "Bearnad."

The afterglow deepened quickly to night, evoking strange cries from the bush. Which was of bird and which of beast I didn't know, but there would be time to learn. Low on the horizon another star appeared— a star so red I thought at first it must be a wing light of an oncoming airplane, but I could hear no engine drone. Instead, a hippo bellowed, another answered, and soon a noisy colloquium was moving up and down the river—groans and roars, complaints and sighs and splashings. The community was preparing to come ashore for its nightly excursion into the long grass, but no one sounded happy about it.

The tropical darkness, permeated by mopani smoke, settled upon my shoulders. I had awoken this morning in a Holiday Inn in Lusaka, and before the day was over I had focused my camera upon the eye of an elephant. Now the pandemonium of hippopotamuses mingled with the muddy odors of the waters in which they lived, steeping me in the Africa I had sought.

AFTER SUPPER we gathered around the fire, and those of us who weren't Muslims sipped amarula, a cream brandy made from the fruit of the marula tree. The early-winter night was clear and chilly, the fire inviting. While hippos bellowed from the river, Harry and Karim told us stories of dangerous game. Harry had been mauled by a lion the year before. An observer had caught the action on video, and Steve had bought a cassette at the SCI convention. I had watched it before we left home, but I wanted to hear the story from Harry himself.

"We were checking a lion bait," he said, "and came upon a big, black-maned lion feeding on it in the middle of the day. The lion moved off, retreated toward heavy cover, and I was looking around to see where to build the blind because they will always come back just before dark, and before I knew it the client shot."

I remembered the scene, the long, ill-advised shot that struck the lion in the gut and the heavy swinging lope of the animal as it disappeared into long grass. Thus far, Harry's account was an exact re-enactment of Hemingway's "Macomber" story, but at this point the script changed. Unlike Hemingway's craven character, Harry's client insisted on going into the bush at Harry's side. An apprentice PH joined them. The three men spread out.

Relating the story, Harry said nothing of the way he had felt as they approached the grass. In the video he had whispered to the client, "move two steps to the left." The lion growled and charged, exploding out of the grass ten steps in front of them, and chose Harry as its victim. He and one of the others got off shots, striking the lion in the upper jaw and in the shoulder, but the lion never flinched. Harry thrust his rifle sideways into the lion's mouth. The lion ripped it from his hands, knocking him down, and seized him by the calf. Neither of the others could shoot for fear of hitting Harry, but the client rushed over to the lion and stuck his rifle in its ear and fired. The four-hundred-pound cat collapsed on Harry's badly torn leg.

The video offered an instant replay of that scene, again and again, in slow motion and stop action, from the initial charge to the killing of the lion—six seconds in real time.

I wondered how often Harry had told the story. Enough to wear away the edges, as much handling rubs away the image on the face of a coin. Like the video, his account was packaged, neatly framed, and the lion could no more jump out of it than it could leap from a TV screen. Although Harry had costarred in the event and could speak with the authority of a survivor, the lion in his account was merely generic. Then Harry said, "Two things I will never forget—how the lion's breath stank in my face, and the yellow eyes when the lion charged. I have never seen anything as cold as those eyes. I still see them. I will always see them." And with that the lion leaped. I could almost feel the pain of the dark puncture scars on Harry's calf.

OUR BEDS were draped at night in veils of mosquito netting. During the day the net was spiraled into folds on its rack overhead, but just before we came in from the bush, servants had let it down and tucked it in around the mattress, forming a tent. There was a feeling of security in sleeping so enclosed, though the security was false. After I crawled in under my tent, baboons just outside the compound began to screech and hoot and howl with a tone of self-righteous indignation that made me smile. Perhaps a prowling leopard had disturbed them. In spite of the bedlam I got to sleep around ten, then woke up at midnight and lay awake for an hour listening to the rising yips of hyenas and watching the wheeling, unfamiliar constellations that I could see through the opening between the wall and the roof. Blacker than the night were the bare limbs of a dead mopani tree silhouetted against the sky.

▼ ▼ ▼

IMPATIENT to get into the bush, I could generate little enthusiasm for Steve's shoe project. For the same reason, I am reluctant to postpone further the beginning of this narrative of hunting in order to recount our visit to a local village. But Steve's arms, which had finally been located in Harare by South Africa Air, would not arrive at the airport until the afternoon flight from Lusaka. So we had a day to kill and eight bags of tennis shoes clumped in the corner of the dining hut.

A traditional village in the Luangwa Valley comprises a small group of families related to each other matrilineally. The residents are usually women and children who tend small plots of maize and sorghum while the men go off to the cities looking for work. The Upper Lupande Game Management Area is closed to settlement and bordered on two sides by the South Luangwa National Park so there were no villages close to our camp. There was, however, a settlement of game scouts near the park's Milyoti Gate, five miles to the north. Created by the government for scouts assigned to the area, it was larger and more prosperous than a typical village. The scouts acted in the capacity of game wardens, collecting entry fees to the park, going out on antipoaching patrols, accompanying tourists on photographic safaris, and monitoring hunts. But the families who lived in the village were as barefooted as most rural Zambians.

We pulled up in two vehicles at a black-and-white barrier just as the early sun was beaming through the treetops. A woman appeared from the gatehouse and swung the bar open, smiling and waving. The road ran through the middle of the village. On both sides, walls of bundled thatch five feet high screened the huts, but from our high perch on the back of the Land Cruiser we were able to see over the walls right down into the morning lives of the people. In front of every hut a cooking fire was burning. Blue mopani smoke plumed in the rays of the sun and permeated the chill air with its distinctive odor. Clean clothes hung stiff on lines strung between huts, and chickens pecked in the dust among blackened wash pots. There were arched doorways in the grass wall opening onto the road. At each of these, small groups of women and children had gathered, anticipating our arrival. They had been told the day before that Americans at the safari camp would come in the morning bringing shoes. Now they had heard the vehicles and gathered to welcome us. We were received by smiles and clapping hands.

We parked beneath an ancient baobab that grew in the midst of the wall. Its smooth gray bark hung in sheets that resembled melted wax. By the time we had descended from the Land Cruiser, the women had plopped down their children on bare dirt in kindergarten order and spread woven grass mats for the display of shoes. A couple of our men brought forth the black duffels and with a flourish dumped out the contents—a tumbling pile of Nikes and Adidas and Reeboks. The eyes of the mothers widened at the extravagance. Immediately they went to work, arranging shoes in rows according to size. Two or three had little ones slung from their hips; another had opened her blouse to her baby; yet another was so great with child that I was afraid she might give birth before we left. Undeterred by these burdens, the women worked quickly and quietly, bending from their high waists with extraordinary flexibility. In a matter of minutes the chaotic pyramid had been reduced to neat rows of mated pairs.

The camp-in-charge, a thin, smiling man in a crisp olive uniform and polished combat boots, stepped forward. Holding a clipboard before him, he began calling out in a loud, military voice the names of the families of the village. The women stood in a still row, arms folded, but the bright prints of the various fabrics they had wrapped around themselves seemed to leap and dance in kaleidoscopic color. One was wearing a skirt that bore the image of President Chiluba stretched across her bottom. One by one, as their names were called, they came forward, shyly making their choices. The children neither stirred nor complained. A three-year-old girl in a frock of blue and magenta, which did not conceal her dirty little underpants, found in her lap a pair of shoes at least two sizes too big for her, white, padded shoes with thick soles and red stripes—the most advanced footwear western technology could produce. She did not touch them but regarded them with great wonderment, as though they were some weird fruit fallen from the sky.

The men had gathered under a tree some distance away, as though to make it clear that children's shoes were women's concern. As the distribution proceeded, they lit cigarettes and joked quietly among themselves. From time to time, one of them would call out to one of the women, saying something that caused the others to double over with laughter. Whatever was going on now did not include us.

As Stuart videotaped the activity, Steve brought out bags of candy—Tootsie Rolls, Jolly Ranchers, bubble gum. The children broke ranks and crowded around him, the older ones as tall as he was. Steve moved among them like a small-town Santa Claus dispensing gifts as the children reached out and cried, "Sweeti, sweeti." In the melee a toddler was bumped to the ground, but before she could gather breath to howl an older girl, no more than six, swung her up onto her hip and popped a piece of gum into her mouth.

The little girl in the blue and magenta dress had thrust her dusty feet into her new oversized shoes, but she could not make them stay on. When she tried to walk, one or the other kept slipping off. The children whose shoes had been laced and tied by their mothers made a show of stomping about, but others held their treasures to their chests. One little boy wore a T-shirt with the smiling face of Dale Earnhardt on the front.

In the mopani woods around the camp gray and yellow-billed hornbills sailed from tree to tree, their long, skinny bodies flattened like kites.

As Steve continued to hand out *sweeti,* I found myself with little to do. Snapping pictures made me feel like a tourist, an intrusive one at that, but Stuart was panning his video back and forth across the smiling faces of these people and no one seemed to mind. What troubled me was the question of whether or not the villagers really needed shoes. It was obvious that they wanted them. They were delighted to get them. But winters here are not cold and they had lived happily barefooted from the dawn of their lives.

Steve had suggested before we left Georgia that he and Stuart and I begin each morning sharing a brief devotional. On this, our first morning in camp, I had found that he was serious. For my part I recited Gerard Manley Hopkins's poem "God's Grandeur." Now as these children tried walking in their new shoes, I recalled the lines,

> Generations have trod, have trod, have trod,
> And all is seared with trade; bleared, smeared with toil;
> And wears man's smudge and shares man's smell; the soil
> Is bare now, nor can foot feel, being shod.

Hopkins is speaking of the obliteration of nature by the industrial West. Now the West had come to Africa and in the goodness of its heart put expensive cross-training shoes on these dusty black feet, introducing something artificial between their soles and the earth, something which, at least in its symbolic ramifications, might do as much damage to the owners of the feet as to the earth they trod.

Somewhere in the back of my head a voice was whispering, "You smug, patronizing bastard. Why complicate the purity of Steve's impulse? Out of the excess of American *stuff* he's giving shoes to barefooted people. It's as simple as that." But before I had time even to flinch at my self-recrimination, Steve was shouting to me, "Get your crosses, Doc."

I had none to get. I had left the bags he'd given me back in camp. On purpose. Shoes were one thing, but I did not feel comfortable distributing pocket crosses to people I did not know. What if they didn't want them? Would they say so or simply accept them because that was the polite thing to do? To answer those questions, I would have to spend time among them, maybe as long as a year, learning their language, earning their trust.

Harry had told us that the Kunda were Christian, but I didn't know what that meant in this cultural context. These tribesmen were only three and four generations removed from people David Livingstone encountered when he crossed the Luangwa Valley. Since then untold numbers have learned to read in mission schools and received treatment in Catholic and Protestant clinics, but it's hard to tell what kind of Christianity has taken root in Livingstone's wake. There are churches of several Christian denominations throughout the country, but sociologists call the religion of rural Zambia syncretism—an amalgam of animism, ancestor worship, and the Gospel. Though missionaries introduced evangelical and antiwitchcraft movements years ago, many of the tribes have adapted Christianity to their cultural traditions. It's not unusual for a man to attend an Apostolic church on Sunday morning and then that afternoon pour homemade beer and mealie meal into a gourd to appease his ancestors. Nor has faith in the presence of the risen Christ banished capricious spirits from the bush. On the other hand, the noted scholar Harvey Cox reports in his recent book *Fire from Heaven* that a Bible-based pentecostalism, unmixed with ancestor worship, is spreading rapidly throughout sub-Saharan Africa.

Whatever one's religious experience, it wears a mask provided by the culture in which one lives. I could no more see through theirs than they could see through mine; but suppose beneath our masks we were brothers and sisters in Christ. I would have liked to know that, but the hour we had was not enough time to find out such things about each other. As we prepared to leave, the people of the village gathered around us. We discovered quickly that their way of shaking hands was different from ours. They were amused by my clumsy effort to figure out how to place my thumb. Then the women began to clap and chant, a high ululation that soon broke off in self-conscious laughter.

Steve came over to where I was standing. "See that little guy in the green shorts? Know what his name is?"

"No, what?"

"I am."

"I am?"

"That's what he said. He came up to me and said, 'I am. How are you?'"

The little girl in the blue and magenta dress suddenly appeared at my side. I put my hand on her head and felt against my palm her tight little springy braids. She looked up, all big eyes, and I blessed her with all my heart.

On our way to the airport to pick up Steve's bows and rifles, we stopped at a rural public school to distribute the rest of the shoes. The buildings were made of brick—two long, low rows of classrooms with casements but no windows, portals but no doors. The blackboards were so scratched and battered that one would have had trouble writing on them, even if chalk had been available. Nor was there electricity. Yet the rooms were filled with students, boys and girls from first grade through high school, and they were dressed as well as their parents could afford—blue dresses and red ties for the girls, white shirts and red ties for the boys. When we drove up, they rushed from their hot, dark dens and crowded around us in the glare of the sun. I saw immediately that we did not have enough shoes to go around. Not nearly enough.

Children danced and yelled as our men emptied the duffel bags. As the pile grew, the circle around the shoes closed in, and the yelling grew louder. Teachers were having trouble controlling the mob until the head teacher arrived and established order. Speaking to them in the language of their tribe, he sent them back to their rooms with the promise that their American friends would visit every class. Then, with several assistants, he divided the shoes into groups corresponding to the number of classrooms. The open windows were crowded with boys and girls trying to see.

In each classroom the teacher and an administrative assistant called out the names of students—the star pupils, they explained to us. One by one the students came forward—girls mostly—and received their rewards with little curtsies. Perhaps a fourth of each class received shoes. Those who did not were given candy and crosses. While we were passing up and down the rows handing out these things, a gangly boy of twelve or thirteen was struggling valiantly to force his wide dusty feet into a pair of polished loafers.

Back at the Land Cruiser, Steve's eyes were glistening. "We should have brought more," he said. "And books. Did y'all see any books? I want to come back with boxes of books."

▼ ▼ ▼

THE FLUORESCENT LIGHT overhead flickered on, and there through the gauzy screen of mosquito netting was Bernard, dressed in starched white and kneeling at a tray on the cement floor, pouring coffee. I couldn't tell if it was light outside or not. I looked at my watch: 5:30. Karim had told me that the servants would feel honored to be addressed in their language so I was prepared. "Mwauka bwanji," I said. Good morning. How are you today? Bernard clasped his hands, bowed, and smiled. "I am well, sir," he answered, amused by my clumsy pronunciation. I pulled the netting from the mattress and sat up to receive the coffee he had prepared. "Zikomo," I said. "Zikomo kwambiri, Bernard."

The eastern sky changed quickly from gray to rose to crimson. Vervet monkeys scampered in the treetops overhead, the branches their highways. I walked about beneath the canopy with my second cup of coffee, craning my neck to watch the activity, reminded of those picture games in which images are hidden in foliage. When I stood still, monkeys materialized, sitting on their haunches in the crotches of trees, their black faces peering down in profound interest, as though they had never seen such naked primates as we were. When I moved, the monkeys disappeared. I was surprised that they had not grown tamer or at least more confiding, living above an abundant supply of food and a camp of people who meant them no harm. But they kept to the topmost branches.

Dawn was loud with the calls of turtle doves, and squadrons of yellow-billed storks flew out over the river.

I joined others at the table and drowned a bowl of cornflakes in heavy cream. Between bites I asked Karim, "What's the game plan for today?"

Deferring to Harry, who had already left the table, Karim replied, "Harry will say."

Harry said hippo.

The standard method for hunting lions is to hang bait from a tree, check it a time or two each day for lion activity, and when spoor is detected build a tree blind, or *machan*, within shooting range, and wait. The most easily acquired large bait animal is the hippo. A big bull may weigh two tons or more. Quartered, he provides bait for several sites for at least a week. Shooting a hippo was the first order of business.

There were always a few of the huge mammals to be seen in the stretch of river in front of the camp, but Steve wanted to take a bull with his bow, a method that would require a much closer shot than the river afforded. Though most of the tributary streams were drying up, Harry had located a pool several days before that had held a large bull. He trusted that it would still be there.

Many people are surprised to learn that the hippopotamus is one of the two or three most dangerous creatures in Africa, accounting for a high percentage of human fatalities caused by animals. They spend the daylight hours mostly submerged in rivers and lagoons, which protect their sensitive skin from the sun, but at dusk they emerge from the water to feed all night on grass. It takes that much to keep them going. Trouble occurs when a person on foot blunders into a hippo in the dark or inadvertently cuts the animal off from its escape route back to water. In spite of its short legs and enormous bulk it can outrun most people over a short distance, especially in the thick vegetation where it feeds, and its tusks, designed for fighting rather than eating, can easily shear a man in half.

The hunt proposed by Harry, even though it would require an approach to within twenty-five yards, presented no significant danger, for he expected to find the animal in water, where it was most vulnerable. What he did not expect with confidence was that Steve's arrow would penetrate the inch-thick hide deep enough to kill.

In the cool, early light, we climbed into the Land Cruiser, observing the same seating arrangement we had established the day before. The trackers Demetrius and Silas had loaded the weapons cases, hanging them from gun racks mounted before the bench seat. For the three of us sitting there, the overlapping cases formed a kind of dashboard or barrier. At our feet was a cooler packed with sandwiches and drinks. The trackers, clad in dark green coveralls, climbed into the back compartment, where they would stand as we rode, looking out for game.

Jason Stone, the young apprentice PH from South Africa, was not a member of Harry's staff, I had learned, but worked for a professional hunter who was currently arranging a safari in Zimbabwe. That morning, Jason was biding his time at Harry's camp, waiting for a call on the radio. Whether or not he would have joined us for the hippo hunt, I would never know, for he was suffering an attack of chronic malaria that had put him to bed. I regretted his absence, not only because of his easy, congenial manner but also because of his knowledge of birds. With Harry concentrating on the hunt, I was on my own as to identification. To that end, I had brought in my day-pack Kenneth Newman's *Birds of Southern Africa*. But on this clear morning I was seeing unfamiliar species faster than I could track them down in the guide. The most common birds were ones I already knew—the sparrow weavers, whose globular straw nests festooned bare limbs all along the road, glossy blue-black starlings, hornbills, and doves. Harry said that five or six species of dove occurred in the valley at this time of year. The most abundant by far was the turtle dove, but the diminutive emerald-spotted dove, reminiscent of our ground dove, was common, and often enough the beautiful na-maqua with its long tail and black mask and throat flew up from the roadside, attracting our attention by its darting acrobatics.

For pure intensity of color no bird could rival the lilac-breasted roller, which revealed in flight wing stripes and tail of a living azure. They were common in the combretum thickets, perched on exposed branches and flying as we approached. As often as I was to see them during the next three weeks, I never grew tired of the brilliance of that blue. Nor of the green of the lovebirds. My first sighting of this species occurred as we were headed north toward the hippo pool. From bare, burnt ground on the left, a large flock of the miniature parrots flushed in a shrill, chattering cloud of sparkling green. These were the Nyasa, or Lillian's, lovebirds, of a neon green and with faces the color of tangerine. There must have been a couple of hundred in the flock, and when they flew, they wheeled in sync, compelled by the same impulse.

WE WERE DRIVING north on the road that runs through the Milyoti Gate village. When we stopped at the gatehouse, a woman in the olive uniform of the game scouts opened the bar. She was the same one who had helped with the distribution of shoes the day before. Always grinning, she had a slightly wall-eyed cast in her left eye that together with her smile gave her a wild, playful look. Harry said she too was a scout, the only female scout in the village.

As we eased past the gatehouse, children emerged from behind grass walls on both sides of the road, hands extended, begging, "sweeti, sweeti." The little boy in green shorts came around to Steve's side. "I am," he said. "How are you?" Steve looked at me and smiled. While he was doling out candy, a man joined Demetrius and Silas in the back of the Land Cruiser. He carried a battered rifle, the front sight of which had been welded on. He was Mbuluma, the scout who would accompany us each day.

"Bwanji, Mbuluma," we said.

The language Harry and Karim spoke in talking with the people who lived near the camp is a central African counterpart of the East African Swahili, a universal pidgin called Nyanja. According to Karim, it is a corrupted version of the language of the people of Lake Nyasa. Traders from the coast, needing to communicate with tribes they encountered in the interior, transported it from Nyasaland (now Malawi) to Mozambique, where it acquired local flavor before spreading west to the Rhodesias. Though it varies in vocabulary and pronunciation from one area to another, it resembles sufficiently most of the seven major tongues in Zambia as to be generally intelligible. Karim grew up in Livingstone, speaking it as a kind of street patois. I wanted to learn as much of it as I could in the short time I had, especially the names of animals.

THE TERM "observer," used in the context of safari hunting, is a negative designation. All it means is "not the hunter." Steve had equipped Stuart and me with fine cameras, and our observing was to be done through the lenses so that friends back at home might observe at second hand the successes of the client. That was fine with me. I considered it the price of admission, a way of seeing animals, and now that Steve was actually hunting, a medium by which I might experience the thrill of the chase without assuming whatever responsibility might be involved in getting blood on my hands.

A herd of impala raced to cross the road up ahead of us but at the last instant broke at the very edge into indecisive individuals. Several of them launched themselves into flight, floating almost over the vehicle, with that gravity-defying ease that has to be seen to be believed. Others spun and wheeled, pulling up in sudden arrest, then pronking away. Far out across the plain, in the shadow of a baobab, a band of zebras stood and watched.

I can't say why the bows and rifles made a difference, why the possibility of blood changed things. But it did. The air was purer, charged with the dry odors of the bush, and I believed that from moment to moment the world as it was made might be revealed ever more fully in the colors and the textures that composed the muted tapestry of the landscape.

We turned left into the bush. Any sign of a track soon disappeared among combretum shrubs, and we were lurching and jouncing over hard, broken ground. I grabbed my camera to keep it from swinging against the gun cases that hung across our front. We went on that way for a long time. I had little sense of distance covered. Once Harry pointed off to the left and announced, "Tawny eagle." On a high limb a large raptor in silhouette. Then he was pulling up beneath a tree that stood in the corner of a wide, wet meadow, and we found ourselves face to face with a pride of lions. There were five of them peering out of long grass. We must have disturbed their naps. They did not seem inclined to move. Harry gunned the engine and eased forward. Karim drew a rifle from its case and checked the chamber. One by one the lions rose and slunk away, grudgingly looking back. One was a big female, the others, I assumed, her grown cubs. One had a fringe of mane. I was snapping pictures as fast as I could, but the cats did not go far. In thicker grass forty yards away they settled in again.

No lion I had ever seen in zoo or circus prepared me for that encounter. Although we were in no danger as long as we remained in the vehicle, the yellow eyes of a wild lion, even when he is sleepy, can make you feel more looked at than you have ever felt.

The wind shifted and I gagged. Ten feet away, hanging against the trunk of the tree where we had stopped, was the hindquarter of a hoofed animal. Though it was covered by a skirt of grass, I could tell that it was big enough to have come from a creature the size of a cow. In the excitement of the lions I had not noticed it, but with the change of wind it would not be denied. It was the hindquarter of a buffalo, about four days old. That's what had attracted the lions and kept them in the neighborhood. Harry and the trackers walked over to the bait, lifted the grass skirt, and examined it for spoor. The hindquarter was hung just high enough that a lion could reach it with his front paws if he extended himself full length. In so doing, an adult male would leave strands of mane stuck to the meat. That's what Harry was looking for. When he returned to the vehicle, Steve asked, "Where's the big boy?"

"Hard to say. Could be on a kill or patrolling his territory, or he could be watching us right now."

The hippo pool was on the far side of the meadow, but the ground was too soft to drive across, and the lions were still too close for us to approach the pool on foot. Harry backed around, circled the meadow until he came to dry ground, then nosed the Land Cruiser into the long grass, which lay before us as smooth as water. But the calm surface concealed a rough bottom. The vehicle lurched and swayed, found holes and deep ditches. When we stopped at last and climbed out, I saw why. The ground was black cotton, the infamous soil that becomes when wet a gummy, sucking porridge but when dry hardens into cement, holding the myriad tracks and trails of buffalo, elephant, and hippo.

The hippo pool was empty. Harry scratched his head. The young lions watched from their edge of the meadow. One sat on its haunches thirty yards away. "Cheeky chap," Karim said.

The empty pool meant that Steve would have to take a hippo from the river with a rifle—a disappointment, but it was a lion he really wanted and the hippo was a means to that end. There was no time to waste driving around the countryside looking for bait that might be vulnerable to an arrow. We headed back to camp.

Along the way a herd of impala crossed the road up ahead. "Real meat," as Harry had said.

Providing meat for the camp, including a large safari staff, is the responsibility of the client, a circumstance that imparted to the hunt the primitive necessity of success. His priority may be a trophy head, but when the trophy is buffalo or almost any of the antelopes, a well-fed camp is a by-product of the hunt. Steve had two impala on his license. Knowing that a successful stalk with bow and arrow would be unlikely because of the wariness of the animal in the open country which is its habitat, he accepted Harry's suggestion that he use a rifle to take a young buck for the pot.

Harry removed a small tin from his breast pocket and sprinkled a fine powder into the breeze. Satisfied that the air was moving in our direction, he headed into the brush. Steve followed, carrying the .300 Weatherby magnum. Next came Stuart with the video, then the trackers and the game scout. Karim and I brought up the rear. I was not sure that I was expected to go along. Or wanted. Many professional hunters, I was told, have little patience with photographers in the bush, especially when the presence of an additional person jeopardizes himself or others or compromises the chances of success. The more people involved in a stalk, the more noise and movement. Harry had agreed to our cameras, but I did not know him well enough yet to have developed a sense of conduct appropriate to the situation. But Karim had motioned to me to follow him.

The country was open. Harry was easing forward in a crouch, carrying the shooting sticks—a bamboo tripod that is easily opened and folded—and the whole party crouched along behind. We must have resembled a crippled caterpillar inching through the grass. From time to time Harry would stop, signaling with his hand for the entourage to halt, but, like the predator he had become, he kept his eyes fixed on the herd of impala. Suddenly, with smooth, decisive movements, he set the tripod and stepped aside for Steve to shoot. Steve placed the rifle on the sticks, aimed, and fired. At the report of the rifle, the herd scattered like a covey of quail, but one animal lunged and staggered. Silas and Demetrius broke into a sprint. Harry clapped Steve on the back and said, "Good shot."

For the sake of the Muslims in camp, the animal had to be "koshered"—its throat cut and blood spilled while it was still alive or as soon after death as possible.

The trackers returned, barefooted Silas carrying the young buck across the back of his shoulders, holding it by its legs, as a shepherd carries a lamb. I stepped aside to get a photograph. The horned head swung against the tracker's back as he walked, and the legs of his dark green coveralls were shiny with blood. The musk of the young animal, stronger than I expected, drifted in his wake, and I wished I had a camera that could preserve that too.

Back in camp, Harry and Steve walked out to the river, Stuart and I in tow. Between the compound and the water lay a beach of white sand two hundred yards wide, blinding in the midday sun. The surface was a thin crust that broke beneath our feet, slowing our progress. Harry stopped and scanned the river for hippo. I squinted against the glare. A small group of Egyptian geese made way for us as we approached the edge of the water. Harry set the shooting sticks, and Steve sighted through the scope of the .375 Holland and Holland. Halfway across, the heads of two hippos broke the surface, facing upriver, and the current streamed behind them in streaks of light. On a sandbar across the river lay three huge crocodiles.

How on earth did Harry plan to retrieve a four-thousand-pound animal from that wide water? Curiosity kept me standing in the blaze of the sun.

Steve fired. Flocks of waterfowl up and down the river rose gabbling at the sound of the shot, which echoed off the far bank. But out in the stream all was still. Both animals had disappeared.

"Good shot," Harry said. "You hit him just behind the eye."

"I was aiming at his nose," Steve explained.

Out of nowhere six or eight young men were standing at the edge of the water. Four of them removed their shirts and waded in. One carried the end of a rope. Balancing themselves against a surprisingly strong current, they eased forward. Their wet backs ranged in hue from an almost purple black to rich chocolate, and their corded muscles rippled with light. Less than halfway across, they were in up to their chests.

Harry and Karim were observing the action through binoculars. "No danger from crocs?" I asked Karim.

Without lowering his glasses, he said, "Not much. The shot scared them off."

"Hippos too?"

"Probably, but we need to keep our eyes open."

"They don't seem worried."

By now the muddy brown current was swirling around their necks. I did not see how they were able to stand against it. "I guess they can swim," I said.

"No," Karim said.

I raised my binoculars. The men must have located a sandbar for the water now was only waist-deep. They had found the hippo too. Why it had not drifted downstream, I did not know, unless the carcass had grounded on the bar where the men were standing. They were attaching the rope to some part of the submerged animal. One of them waved, and the men on shore began to pull. The dripping rope slowly lifted from the water, sagging with its own wet weight. The men leaned into the work, a fierce tug against the Luangwa River current and two tons of dead meat. The men in the river pushed and rolled the hippo. Harry and Karim joined the team on the bank, then Steve took a place at the rope. Little by little, the monstrous catch was drawn to shore. When at last it lay in the shallows, it was a rope's length downstream, swept that far by the current.

Without water to float the carcass, the men were unable to roll it onto the beach. Harry sent someone to get the Land Cruiser.

Lying on its back in the shallows, the hippo lost its familiar form and spread out like a vast balloon filled with water, a balloon with four short round legs, flopping outward. The muddy umber of its flanks faded to a leprous, mottled pink on the belly. I placed my palm against its roundness, and it offered no more resistance than dough.

When the vehicle arrived, Harry uncoiled the winch cable and attached it to the rope, the other end of which was fastened around the hippo's neck. He switched on the winch and the line tightened, stretched to its utmost. The motor screamed. I didn't know which would go first, the winch or the line. Then grudgingly the carcass yielded to the machine. Landed at last, it made an enormous pile.

Steve wanted to prove to Harry that the eighty-eight-pound pull of his compound bow would penetrate the hippo's thick hide. He backed off thirty yards, pointed the bow straight toward the sky, and with a great effort drew back the arrow. Aiming through the sight, he released it. The broadhead struck the dead animal just back of the shoulder and buried itself to the fletching. When Steve wrenched the arrow free, blood pulsed from the wound, streaming down the hippo's side and reddening the wet sand.

Two of the men grasped the upper jaw of the hippo, one on either side, working their hands between the tough, rubbery lips, and forced open the mouth, wide at the front, narrowing towards the throat. Another jammed a stick inside to hold it open. The curved tusks were stained dark, the lower pair so long that when the mouth was closed they pushed against the upper lip, creating the bumps outside the nostrils by which one tells that the animal is a mature bull. Between them and protruding straight forward from the floor of the mouth is another set. The front teeth of the upper jaw are not as long but there are eight of them, all sharp spikes. I grasped one of the lower tusks. It filled my hand.

With those weapons, it is said, a hippo can inflict mortal wounds upon a rival bull or bite a canoe in half. Yet for all that fearsome equipment, hippos are vegetarian, a diet for which its tusks are useless. Harry called my attention to the lips. "That's how he clips grass," he said. When one considers the fibrous toughness of the stems, the strength of the lips is surely one of the animal's most impressive features.

I was called on to take the obligatory trophy pictures, though this bloated sausage of a creature seemed little more than a mountain of lion bait. Steve and Harry knelt behind it.

For the same reason that I did not regard the hippo as a trophy, I felt no compunction in its death. The killing of it was easy enough to justify by the necessity of controlling the population against outbreaks of anthrax, which tends to strike when hippos congregate in great numbers. But such practical considerations did not explain my indifference. What did was the animal's lack of nobility—a scruple that convicted me of anthropomorphizing sentimentality. I don't think I would be able to bear the killing of an elephant, nor was I altogether comfortable with the hunting of cats. But by what accounting are lions and elephants of greater meaning than hippos?

It so happens that God has an opinion on the matter. Here is what he says to Job:

> Behold now behemoth, which I made with thee; he eateth grass like an ox.
>
> Lo now, his strength is in his loins, and his force is in the navel of his belly.
>
> . . . .
>
> His bones are as strong pieces of brass; his bones are like bars of iron.
>
> He is the chief of the ways of God: he that made him can make his sword approach unto him.
>
> . . . .
>
> Behold, he drinketh up a river and hasteth not: he trusteth that he can draw up Jordan into his mouth. (Job 40, selected verses, KJV)

Chief of the ways of God? Not by any standard familiar to me. Which is, I suspect, God's point.

▼ ▼ ▼

BEFORE LEAVING for Africa, I had told my daughter Sarah Jane that Steve would be hunting lion, leopard, and buffalo.

"Lion and leopard too? Why?"

Sarah Jane had grown up around men who hunted. From early childhood she had watched me clean ducks and deer in the back yard, and she had eaten venison as often as beef. Though she had never expressed interest in learning to hunt herself, she had applauded her brother's early successes in the field, and her understanding of what I can only call the mystique had survived intact as she became an adult. But when she asked me why—why shoot a lion or a leopard—there was such sincere dismay in her tone that I could find no answer.

"I'm sorry, Daddy, I just can't handle that."

I tried anyway. "To begin with, Sadie, you have to understand that these species are not endangered, not where we're going. Leopards are as common as coyotes, and leopard hunting is carefully monitored and regulated by the Game Department. The hunter has to pay a big fee for a leopard permit, and on top of that he has to get a permit from CITES, which is the Conference on International Trade in Endangered Species, in order to bring the skin into this country. The individual Steve kills will eventually die of old age or injury anyway. From a game management standpoint, he's just culling from the excess."

"I understand all that but why even do it? I mean, what's the purpose of shooting an animal if it's not good to eat?"

Ah, I had taught her well. From her early childhood I had presented her with an ideal of the woodsman who enters the natural world with appreciation for beauty and reverence for life, who seeks to understand the ways of the animal he hunts, who kills only to acquire food, and who does that quickly and humanely. No one had denounced more vehemently than I the slob who shoots to gratify his own ego. The answer to her question was obvious—if one is not going to eat the animal he shoots, he must be hunting for a trophy, but still I tried to evade that unpalatable fact. "It's the hunt, Sarah Jane— entering the domain of a dangerous animal, pitting one's skills, especially with a bow and arrow, against the strength and wariness of a beautiful animal . . . " I broke off, bogged down in the bullshit I was shoveling. "It feels a little funny to me too," I said, "but I still want to be there. I can't explain it."

According to the principles my daughter reminded me of, shooting a zebra was as hard to justify as killing a leopard. Maybe even more so. Zebra skins make striking rugs, and Steve wanted one, but his main purpose in hunting zebra was to secure leopard bait. As a hippo quarter is hung alongside the trunk of a tree to attract lions, part of the zebra carcass would be tied to the underside of a large horizontal branch, for leopards are more comfortable feeding in trees than on the ground.

The zebra of eastern Zambia is the common, or Burchell's, zebra, *Equus burchellii*. The Luangwa Valley race is *E. b. selousi*, named for the great hunter Frederick Courtney Selous. Because there are no vast, open grasslands in the valley, zebra there do not gather in great herds as they do in the Serengeti, nor are they migratory. At the beginning of the dry season, when the long grass is turning brown, game scouts set fire to the savannas and woodlands, burning out old growth and making way for green shoots that spring up across the blackened landscape. On this sparse though tender growth zebras graze in small family groups throughout the dry months. It occurred to me that a skinned carcass would look like that of a horse, which may be God's most eloquent articulation of grace, strength, and beauty uttered in a single word.

IN THE LATE AFTERNOON the trackers in the back of the vehicle spotted a small herd of zebra about three hundred yards off the road. Seeing those boldly striped animals in the bush is not as easy as one might suppose. As soon as a zebra stops moving, the pattern of white and black changes into light and shadow, and the zebra merges into the background. I marveled at what struck me as the trackers' almost telescopic vision, but without that gift Silas and Demetrius would have been working other jobs.

The zebra were grazing in open woodland, appearing and disappearing among trees and shrubs of a wild orchard. Karim handed Steve his bow and a quiver of arrows, which Steve strapped around his hips. Harry led the way. We followed with our cameras at a distance of twenty steps, keeping our eyes on Harry. What he did, we did. When he and Steve stopped and knelt, we hid behind an ant hill—a mound of hard red earth with bushes and small trees growing out of it. I could see nothing in front of me, but Stuart rolled to his left, around the shoulder of the mound, and, lying on his stomach, aimed his camera.

In central Africa darkness falls so swiftly you can almost hear the thud. Steve had less than thirty minutes to get his leopard bait. The sun dropped behind the trees, and a stirring of cool air quickened the smells of the bush. The glare of early afternoon softened to a pale golden light, and not far off an emerald-spotted dove began to call— a haunting song of low, descending coos that had already become one of my favorite African sounds. I lay back against the mound and tried consciously to open wider my eyes, ears, nose, and every pore.

Stuart whispered my name. I rolled toward him and looked out over his shoulder. Three zebra were cropping tender shoots of new grass, moving from left to right, maybe seventy yards away. A mare came into view, a half-grown colt at her side. With the sun setting behind them their forms were traced by light, and the orchard glowed. A stallion followed, pushing the mare and colt ahead. Alert to danger, he sniffed the cooling evening air. I could not tell whether Steve and Harry were within bow range of the animals or not, but the stallion had more to worry about now than the hunter's arrow. "Thou makest darkness," the Psalmist says, "and it is night; wherein all the beasts of the forest do creep forth. The young lions roar after their prey, and seek their meat from God."

It was hard to tell just who was hunting who, or why, but we were all exalted.

On the way back to camp, I sat hunched forward against the cold wind. The headlights struck the masked, raccoonlike face of a sturdy, medium-sized animal, which I recognized as a civet, but a little later I needed Karim's help in identifying a smaller ring-tailed creature that darted across in front of us. "Genet," he said.

The bush was astir with predators.

AFTER SUPPER we spent an hour by the campfire rehashing the events of the day. As we stood up to go to bed, the grass outside the fence rustled. Harry said "Ssh" and switched on his hand-held spotlight. No more than twenty feet away stood a hippo, its monstrous head thrashing the grass in a demonstration of displacement anxiety. Harry said later that it was a female, though its round back was scarred from fighting. "That's the grieving widow of the bull you killed," I told Steve, "and she's come a-looking for you."

▼▼▼

WHEN WE GOT UP the next morning, Harry showed us leopard tracks in the fine dust of the compound. He said the cat was a female. She had entered through the main gate and passed between the wall of the kitchen area and the dining hut, and then bounded over the low wall in front of the dining hut out onto the river beach.

THE SUN was just peeping over the eastern hills when we turned from the main road onto the rough, broken track that led to the lion bait by the hippo pool, but we had not yet removed our jackets. As Harry maneuvered the vehicle along the twisting track, we happened upon a small group of zebra standing in the early light. Harry stopped. The nervous mares edged their colts into cover, but the stallion stood trembling in that paralysis between flight and defense. Steve was already on the ground, nocking an arrow, and I was fumbling with the camera. The zebra was no more than fifty yards away, a long shot for Steve but well within range of my 300-millimeter zoom. I extended the lens, and how those unbelievable stripes rushed into focus, even the intricate pattern around the large, dark, horse's eye. Steve and I shot at the same instant; the zebra bolted, and neither of us knew if we had hit the target.

The trackers went to work, barefooted Silas and Demetrius in a quilted jacket long since faded to pink. They eased forward, four careful eyes scanning the hard, uneven ground for the least red drop, Demetrius as senior tracker a step ahead of his partner, his right arm extended, index finger pointing downward as though like a divining rod it might tingle in the presence of blood.

The drops were tiny and infrequent. The trackers cast back and forth, pausing, examining, moving again, finding the next drop not by sight but by a sense as mysterious to me as the nose of a dog. Harry and Steve meanwhile had swung out in a wide arc, advancing quickly. They were looking for the zebra. Before long they were out of sight.

An hour's search discovered nothing encouraging. Harry and Steve returned from their long scout and conferred with Demetrius. From the scant sign they all agreed that the zebra was not mortally wounded. It was Steve's impression that the zebra, which had stood facing away at a three quarters angle, had turned at the instant of release. The arrow had apparently glanced off the elbow. Perhaps my photograph would confirm the suspicion, but we would be back in Athens before it was developed.

The north-south road through the Upper Lupande Game Management Area crosses a short-grass savanna a few miles beyond the Milyoti Gate village. Burned just before we arrived, it lay in scorched contrast to the dusty gray-green woodlands that surrounded it. Here and there stood skeletons of old mopani trees killed long ago by elephants, and in the center of the landscape a lone baobab. I don't think we ever drove through that plain without seeing zebra. We had come to call it the zebra plain. After Steve missed his shot with the bow, we backtracked to the zebra plain and sure enough a herd of eight or ten were grazing around the baobab. Harry turned from the road and drove out across the flat, bare ground, flushing plovers that cried like killdeers in flight. The zebras in the shade of the baobab trotted away, toward the distant line of woodland. Harry stopped. From here they would go on foot.

Once the hunting party had moved away from the vehicle, the noisy plovers returned, small groups alighting around us. Like members of their family throughout the world, these were distinguished by patterns of black and white on head and neck—specifically, a black cap circled by a white band that suggested a crown. Hence the name—crowned plover—as I learned from my bird guide, which went on to say, "often flies about in small groups at some height calling repeatedly."

Karim had his binoculars fixed on the hunters, growing smaller in the distance.

We sat in the Land Cruiser, at the center of a landscape that showed no sign of civilization. Even the ash was natural. I wondered if Karim and Mbuluma were seeing the same thing I was, or if they were construing the features of the landscape into a hieroglyphic that no one but themselves could interpret. Their views differed from each other's, I suspected, as much as either of them did from mine, for each of us brings to the viewing of country his own experience— limitations and inclinations—and thereby shapes the landscape he observes. Karim was seeing with the eyes of a professional hunter,

Mbuluma with the eyes of a Kunda who had grown up here. Because of their presence, whatever they were seeing, I realized that I was looking only upon the surface. Like bonefishing in the Bahamas, when I was unable to make out the water-colored fish beneath the sun-dappled wavelets, while the Bahamian guide reads the rumpled bottom through a sparkling net of light and shadow, seeing everything, whispering, "Fish coming, eleven o'clock, twenty yards," and I couldn't believe it, couldn't believe that he could see them or that they were really there.

There must have been things happening out there, right before my eyes, that I could not discern.

A shot rang out. Rolling terrain hid the hunters, but the largest herd of hoofed animals I had yet witnessed appeared in the distance—zebra, impala, and wildebeest, thundering across the plain. It almost looked like the Serengeti. Karim and I scanned the scene through binoculars. One zebra was dropping back. Directly, he stopped and stood in the cloud of dust left by the herd.

"That's a sick zebra," Karim said. "Very sick."

Karim meant that the zebra had been hit.

It stood for a long time after the herd had disappeared.

Another shot. Then another. The zebra did not move. "Steve's having a bad day," I said.

The zebra began to walk away. It walked slowly but it did not stumble.

"He paunched him with that first shot," Karim said.

At the sound of the next shot the zebra broke into a labored trot. Another shot. "That one did it," Karim said. "Did you hear it hit?"

The zebra was down. Karim climbed forward into the driver's seat and started the engine. We rolled across a charred hardpan strewn with bones and skulls of zebra and wildebeests. Lion kills. Because of vultures, hyenas, rodents, and fire, even bones do not last long in the bush; these must have been recently dead, and the number was surprising. The clean, dry residue of an endless cycle of carnage, repeated every night. Sooner rather than later Steve's stallion would have fallen to a lion.

The zebra lay on the burnt ground, its legs and the underside of its belly smudged by ash. The pattern of stripes along its spine was unique to this particular animal, never to be repeated. Yet the general idea is impressive enough. In zebras, we are told, nature has spent millennia selecting for a color pattern by which the animal is rendered invisible to lions at night. But look what we get in daylight, when lions are not about—an instance of divine abandon to delight the eye of a child. Who but God would have had the imagination to paint a white horse with black stripes?

Steve wondered at the colors of the muzzle, soot black around the mouth and nostrils, velvety brown ochre on the sides of the nose. He asked Harry if the brown was typical.

"No," said Harry. "Most muzzles are all black, but you do see brown."

He squatted in the ash and stroked the muscled neck. Then he looked up. "These are the colors of Africa," he said. The blood that flowed from the zebra's mouth was dark red and clotted.

The trackers humped the animal onto the back of the Land Cruiser, hind end first, then the shoulders. They folded back the head and neck to get the tailgate closed. Then they brought bundles of grass that they tucked in between the animal and the metal of the vehicle to protect the skin.

HARRY'S PHRASE caught my attention. Had it been printed on a nineteenth-century placard, it would have stood out in bold type with little pointing fingers in the margins. But Harry didn't say it that way. He was not the kind of man who makes proclamations or tosses metaphors about. I, on the other hand, am. I wanted the phrase to mean more than met the ear. Later, I would come upon a book called *Large Mammals and a Brave People* by Stuart Marks, a biologist and anthropologist who had done his Ph.D. work among the Bisa tribe just a few miles north of where we were hunting. In a discussion of the systems by which the Bisa classify animals, Marks lists size, sex, and age, but for the Valley Bisa, he says, "the primary categories are those of color."

As with many other Central African groups, their scheme is based upon a triad of red, black, and white. *Nama ziasweta,* literally "red animals," includes the tawny or khaki mammals such as impala, lion, puku, roan antelope, and hartebeest. . . . Black mammals, *nama ziafita,* form another group which includes the buffalo, rhino, elephant, jackal, ant bear, warthog, and waterbuck.

Occasionally white or albinistic mammals are encountered. Such mammals are considered *mipashi*—protective "presences" which guard the herds with which they run.

All other mammals which have two or more distinct colors on their pelage are grouped as *vizemba.* Included in this category are zebra, leopard, wild cat, bushbuck, kudu, eland, wild dog, cape polecat, and giraffe.

Responding to this system with a Western mind, I assumed that each color signified an arcane native lore about animals, and if I could find out what that was, I would understand the mystery of animals more fully. So, thinking I had missed the key, I reread Marks's paragraph, but after about five times I saw that the only key is the *absence* of any values associated with color. The dominance of the Bisa perception of color challenges our Linnean rage to divide and classify and obliterates such distinctions as predator/prey, good to eat/not good to eat, even the taxonomic categories of cat/dog/pig/horse/goat as primary means of ordering the world.

Steve's zebra was *vizemba,* a combination of the color triad, and Harry had seen in that what he called "the colors of Africa." We were standing beneath a blue sky and surrounded by green foliage, but those hues seemed inconsequential. The sky was changing moment by moment as it would all day until dark and then all night; and the leaves were changing with the onset of the dry season. Bright flowers had faded and fallen, and the leaves were exhausted into dull gray-green. Only the colors of the earth remain constant—black and white, sienna, ochre, and umber. The evolutionary process that selects for protective coloration results in pelage that is fundamental, elemental, marvelously responsive to subtleties of light and shadow—the true colors ancient cave painters achieved by mixing animal fat with red and yellow oxides and ground charcoal and applying the pigments to stone.

▼ ▼ ▼

THE TABLE was covered by a yellow oilcloth with a blue floral print. Down the center, from one end to the other, stood jars of condiments—chutneys, hot sauces, salad dressings. Supper began with a bowl of potato soup served by Bernard and his assistants Victor and Moses, dressed in starched white uniforms.

Steve had killed a baboon with an arrow that afternoon, a big male sitting on the limb of a mahogany tree just outside the compound wall. At forty yards the shot had been his best yet, but all he had to show for it was a baboon after all, a fascinating creature but hardly a noble trophy. Harry was laughing now at how the creature had squealed when the arrow struck.

"You don't like baboons, do you?" Steve asked.

"No," he said. "At another camp where I used to hunt, a troop of baboons would come out every evening onto the roots of a big tree at the edge of the river and taunt the crocs, jumping up and down and howling and throwing things in the water. And almost every day a big croc would lunge out of the river and snatch one. They never learned. *Eeeeee, eeeeee, eeeee,* they would squeal, but they always came back. They just couldn't help it."

In telling that story Harry let his stern mask slip for a moment and I glimpsed something adolescent in his features—a locker-room kid's assumption that we were all buddies sharing his glee in the tribulations of a vile creature. His attitude must have been contagious, for we all laughed with him at the picture he painted.

The servants brought the entree—creamed potatoes and impala stroganoff. Beginning with Steve, they continued around the table to Stuart and me, then to Layla and Harry. Jason and Karim divided what was left.

"What do you plan to do with that thing?" I asked Steve.

"A full-body mount with the leopard attacking it."

The leopard.

Leopards are solitary, nocturnal predators. When a leopard kills, he drags the prey, sometimes weighing twice as much as he does, up into the crotch of a tree so that lions and hyenas can't steal it. Because of those habits, one has to hunt leopards at night. The traditional method involves hanging bait, then checking it for spoor, and when spoor is detected, building a blind. If the client is a bow hunter, as Steve was, the blind must be located much nearer the bait tree than it would be if the hunter were using a rifle. The problem is that in Zambia, as in many African countries, shooting leopard at night is against the law. The hunter's hope is that the cat will come to the bait at sunset or at dawn, when the sky is light enough to silhouette the target. But that's a thin hope. A leopard is very cautious. Because the bait is not a kill he made himself, he is more suspicious than usual. If he comes at all, he is likely to come in the dark.

Professional hunters are equipped with powerful spotlights. I was told that as many as eighty percent accede to their clients' wishes in this matter. Game officials know that and make little, if any, effort to enforce the law.

One might guess that the leopard population has suffered as a result, but the cats are abundant in the Luangwa Valley. In the Upper Lupande GMA only five permits had been issued the year we were there. Each came with a high price tag, and the hunter was also required to show a permit from CITES. Whether a client chose to shoot at night or not, the local leopard population was flourishing.

Dessert was flan. We had almost finished when Demetrius approached the table and whispered to Harry. Harry said, "A leopard is on the bait. We go now."

I was uncertain of our destination, but wherever we were going, we were going on foot. Harry said we would be spending the night in a blind. We were all excited and trying not to show it. Not knowing what to take and having little time to ask, I grabbed the camera and a plastic bag of medicines and fell in line behind the others. Harry led us across the kitchen compound and out the other side into a well-beaten path that ran through grass taller than our heads. I hurried to keep pace with the man in front me—Stuart, I thought—but there was no moon and I stumbled in the dark. We were headed toward the skinning hut below the camp but how far that was I did not know. We walked in silence. The path led gradually downhill. Dark forms of huts stood on a low ridge to our right, maybe staff quarters. Suddenly, we stepped into a miasma of decay, a stench so strong that I wanted to tie my bandanna across my face, but no one else seemed affected so I just tried not to breathe.

Presently, we came upon a campfire. A pot of something white and thick was bubbling on the coals. Harry whispered to one of the men sitting there. The man shook his head. By the weak flicker of flame I could see that we were in a dry streambed, beneath a cavelike canopy, at the foot of a steep embankment. Harry led us up the bank over protruding, twisting roots. At the top we came upon a grass hut and followed Harry into the tiny vestibule. Harry turned on his flashlight. The vestibule was the blind, recently added to the main section. In the opposite wall were two windows, one for the bow and one for the video. Twenty steps beyond the window, chained to a post set in the ground in front of the blind, was the red carcass of what looked like a headless horse. A door to the left opened upon a large room.

Harry aimed the beam of his light through the door, directing us to enter. Much of the dirt floor was covered by three mattresses laid side by side. On each was a pillow and a blanket. At the far end of the room, beyond the last mattress, hung a zebra skin, draped like a sheet over a clothesline, and next to it something small and yellowish, resembling a child's bathing suit, that I took to be the hide of Steve's baboon.

As we chose our places, the flashlight played here and there, revealing along the opposite wall flensed skulls of horned game—buffalo, puku, impala, and waterbuck—trophies of the safari that preceded ours. Skins of two large animals, weighted by a heavy blanket of salt, lay spread beneath the draped zebra hide. We were going to spend the night in this charnel house, and I was choking on the stench. I wondered if that was a sensation one might grow accustomed to.

Arrangements were made in silence. I took the outside berth, furthest from the blind, and found myself stretched out almost directly beneath the clothesline of drying skins. Stuart lay next to me, and then Steve, and then Harry. Once I had made myself comfortable— or as comfortable as possible in that evil-smelling darkness—I discovered that I needed to urinate, which would mean having to crawl across the legs of the others to reach the door. Harry probably would not allow it anyway, because of the human smell, though how a leopard might detect the odor of a small puddle of pee in that foul atmosphere I could not imagine. I resigned myself to my plight, despairing of sleep. A mosquito sang in my ear, reminding me that I had not taken my malaria pill. The travel clinic at the University of Georgia had recommended Larium as a prophylaxis, but possible side effects include depression, nightmares, and paranoia. We had chosen the alternative, a daily dose of the antibiotic doxycycline. The bottle was in my medicine bag, but I had brought no water, and neither had anyone else. I also had a plastic container of insect repellent but figured Harry would object to the scent. I pulled my blanket over my head and soon grew hot.

THERE WAS no large African animal that I was more eager to see than a leopard, probably because it is the gaudiest of the predators and the most elusive. But I didn't want to see one at night caught frozen in a spotlight, like a grizzly at a garbage dump; I wanted to see him stretched out on a limb in dappled shade with his long tail hanging straight down or standing on a rock in the late afternoon. Harry had said at supper that he had not seen a leopard in daylight in two years of hunting, so my chances were not good. And as for a spotlighted leopard, the situation in the blind would not permit me a view anyway. There was room at the windows only for three.

BY QUESTIONING the hunting of leopards, my daughter had afforded me a momentary glimpse of hunting as it is viewed, not by her, but by the vast numbers of people in our society who are insulated from the natural, elemental world, who hate firearms, and enjoy watching animals on TV. Even many who are not so insulated, people such as hikers, canoeists, mountain climbers, and bird-watchers, oppose hunting as senseless slaughter. The question they ask is disarmingly simple: Why do you want to kill a beautiful fellow creature that has done you no harm? Given its premises, that is a question that cannot be answered by rational explanation, but in Zambia, amidst the odors of carnage, it seemed irrelevant. The inescapable odor of decay not only permeated one's clothing, it seeped into the soul as well. It may be too easy to dismiss an argument by saying, "You had to be there." But that is a place to begin. The cycle of life and violent death that governs the natural world everywhere is more immediate in Africa. The sky is never empty of vultures. The roar of a lion at night calls forth in you a response from a place you were not aware of. Words like "primal" and "atavistic" are abstractions; the sensation in your groin is not. Predation is the way of things, as it has been from the beginning, or at least since the ark came to rest on Ararat. Steve and Harry and the trackers participated in it, and their movements came to seem as natural to me as the stalk of a lioness, flattened in grass exactly the color of her coat. I had no desire to shoot a lion or a leopard, but I knew as I lay in that stinking darkness that we are predators too, our very brains the product of countless millennia of stalking meat. The impala I had eaten for supper was no different from the dismembered hippo or the red zebra that were contaminating the air I was trying not to breathe. I wanted the leopard to come.

HARRY STOOD UP and ducked through the door. Steve followed. Thank God, a bathroom break. Unable to find my shoes, I went barefooted. Outside, on the back side of the blind, four men spread out in a line, making sure to leave plenty of space on either hand in the near total darkness, and spattered the dust. On the way back in, Harry asked if anyone had mosquito dope. I produced mine, and just like that, two miseries were relieved. I was soon asleep.

The next thing I knew, Stuart was whispering in my ear, "Wake up, Doc. The leopard. Listen." I heard crunchings and a cracking of bone. Stuart was crawling toward the vestibule where Steve and Harry had taken their positions. Harry switched on the flood, then turned it off. Stuart came back to his mattress. "Hyena," he said.

When I woke again, I could just make out the horned white skulls leaning against the far wall. People were stirring, speaking in low but audible tones. The leopard had come three times during the night, Harry said, but, finding the bait on the ground and the scent of hyenas all about and hearing perhaps our snoring, he had refused to approach.

▼ ▼ ▼

IT WAS STILL DARK when we left the stench of the blind, the abattoir where we had spent the night, but gray dawn as we walked into camp. The river was shining in the early light and monkeys were chattering in the canopy above. I went straight to our chalet, shed my reeking clothes and took a hot shower to wash the stink from my hair and beard. After a quick breakfast of cornflakes, we were off to check lion baits.

Just outside camp we came upon giraffe browsing the sunlit tops of yellow acacia trees. They were right beside the road. Harry stopped the vehicle. There were two of them. I aimed the camera, extended the lens. Then I saw another, a cow with a half-grown calf, their incredible necks long painted stalks among the limbs and ragged foliage. Unconcerned, the animals moved slowly with a peculiarly graceful rocking gait. I finished a roll of film, and lo, standing no more than fifteen feet away was the bull, where he had been all along. The gaudy splotches of chestnut on his neck and shoulders blended perfectly with the camouflage of sunlight and shadow. He towered above us, looking down through sleepy, girlish lids. I hurried to open a box of film.

These were Thornicroft's giraffe (*Giraffa camelopardalis thornicroftii*). A rare subspecies unique to the Luangwa Valley, it was made known to science in the early twentieth century by a district commissioner of that name who sent a skin to the Natural History Museum of London.

The bull that had been standing by the road stepped away with great dignity just as I finished changing film. Then he stopped and turned his face to us. Long strands of saliva, shining in the sun, drooled from his mouth, and I felt that I had entered what Hemingway called "the kingdom of the animals," which is an utterly different thing from the animal kingdom.

On the way to the first lion bait, we passed a grassy seepage in which two long-legged storks were feeding. The birds were boldly patterned in black and white, but their most striking feature was their long, colorful bills—blood red they were with a broad black band halfway down and a peculiar structure of bright yellow overlapping a portion of the upper mandible, as a saddle sits on the back of a horse. Hence the name—saddle-billed stork.

I SPENT THE AFTERNOON in camp catching up on my notes, writing at a bamboo table by the fire pit. Birds on the beach distracted me from time to time, and now and then Bernard or one of the other members of the domestic staff crossed the compound in their rounds of housekeeping. Though they were too well-mannered to let me catch them watching me, I knew that they wondered what I was up to. The observer from America who this afternoon does not observe but sits in camp sipping coffee and scribbling in his notebook.

I had to. If I was to make anything other than a photographic record of the experience, if I was going to write about Africa, I had to steal an occasional afternoon from the bush. In those first days I was more or less constantly intoxicated by sensation, wide awake as I had not been since childhood, and the only way not to miss anything was to get it down on paper and hope to get it right. It was good that I had no time for reflection. If I could catch in language the landscape and the animals in it so that later, back home in Georgia, the words would restore to me the place as I had known it, like that amber-lighted evening when I had lain against the anthill listening to the calls of emerald-spotted doves and watching the small herd of zebra dissolve stripe by stripe into the darkening bush—and the place, evoked, would stir in me feelings that were true, then that would be enough.

With dark a crescent moon as thin as a line drawn in silver ink appeared low in the western sky, out over the river. I sat alone by the fire, sipping a gin and tonic and listening to night creatures waking up. I was vaguely troubled by the concern that three weeks of observation would not provide an experience to write a book about.

AFTER SUPPER Harry, Steve, and Stuart left on foot for the leopard blind. I saw no reason to join them. Whatever might come to the bait, I would be in no position to see it, and my presence would add unnecessarily to any human noise or smell. When the hunters had departed, Harry's wife, Layla, said goodnight. Karim and I poured cups of coffee and went over to the fire, which felt good now that the night had grown cool. We could not see the Southern Cross from where we sat because of the trees, but that did not matter. The night sky glowed with starlight.

"Hear the leopard, Doc?"

"No. How far off?"

"He's in the park, I think."

I listened. A bush baby wailed from a nearby tree and out in the river a hippo bellowed, sounding like a lion to my unpracticed ear, but I heard nothing that might have been described as the ripsaw coughs of a leopard.

What I knew of Karim was little enough. Twenty-eight years old, he had grown up in Livingstone, near the Victoria Falls. He referred to Harry as his uncle; his mother was Harry's first cousin. A Muslim, he was married and the father of a little boy, whom he was missing terribly.

"When will you get to go home?" I asked.

"Not until the end of August. I will have to spend a few weeks seeing about our farm, but I plan to join Harry again in Tanzania in October."

The safari season runs from the first of June until the rains begin in late November. Even with a month-long break, that is a long time for a young man to be separated from his family.

"What made you choose this profession? Did you hunt when you were a boy?"

"Yes. It was a tradition in my family. My great-grandfather was a white hunter. But it was Harry who really inspired me. This is my second year with him. I hope to complete my apprenticeship by the end of the season."

"It must be hard on your family, your being gone so much."

"It is hard for me too, but it would be harder not being in the bush. I missed it too much. It gets in your blood."

Inevitably, I thought of David Livingstone. "Like malaria."

Karim laughed. "Funny that you should mention that."

"Oh no."

"Just a little chill, but I'd better get to bed."

We said goodnight. "Wake me now," I told him, "if Steve gets a leopard."

▼ ▼ ▼

THE LEOPARD HUNTERS came in about 6:30. They were all quiet. Harry looked sick. Steve said, "We had an event."

The leopard had come just before daylight. Harry woke Steve who moved straight to the window and drew his bow. Harry switched on the light and there crouched a big tom, fifteen steps away. Harry whispered, "Take him." Steve, who was not accustomed to being told by another person when to release an arrow, lost his concentration and shot too soon. The leopard grunted and ran. Steve and Stuart thought the arrow went over the cat's back. Harry thought the leopard was hit. After breakfast they were going into the bush to see what they could find.

"HARRY doesn't understand the way we hunt," Steve told me. He meant that Americans are not accustomed to hunting with guides. We go into the woods alone, hunt at our own pace, and make our own decisions as to when and what to shoot. That style of hunting is not possible for a safari client in Africa because of the dangers of the bush. Steve understood that. But until he and Harry learned to think as one, such mistakes as the leopard shot were bound to happen. Harry was not at fault. He was doing his job. But his decision to speak disrupted the rhythm of Steve's concentration. When Harry whispered, "Take him!" he meant, "That's the leopard you want." But Steve, who had drawn the bow, understood Harry to mean, "Take him now!" and released the arrow a split second before he had the cat lined up in his sight. Whatever the species of game, whether a bird in flight or a cautious buck in switch cane, there comes an instant in hunting when the chance for an effectual shot is better than it has been or will be—the optimal moment—and the experienced hunter recognizes it. That instant had not coincided with Steve's eye and hand when he released the arrow.

"Harry thinks I wounded the leopard," Steve told me, "but the arrow went right over his back."

AFTER BREAKFAST we rode down to the skinning hut—the first time I had seen the area in daylight. The zebra rib cage chained to the stake had been gnawed down to white bone. As Harry, Karim, Steve, and the trackers combed the area for blood, they kept their thoughts to themselves. No one seemed eager to enter the thick riparian forest. The white hunter J. A. Hunter, who lived in Kenya during the first half of the twentieth century, writes in his memoir that the leopard is the most dangerous of the big five, which also includes elephant, lion, buffalo, and rhino. Peter Capstick, who hunted concessions in the Luangwa Valley, agreed, provided that the leopard was wounded. Unlike a gut-shot lion which may or may not charge from cover, a sick leopard can be counted on to charge, and to charge without a warning growl. Hunter and Capstick, as well as other outdoor writers, report that the wounded leopard waits perfectly concealed, focusing his yellow eyes on the approaching hunter. When the man is within certain range, the leopard strikes with the speed of a cobra. Capstick, given a bit to hyperbole, says that by the time you see him he's already within a few inches of your nose, the claws of his front feet reaching for your throat, his pinwheeling hind legs unbuckling your belt. Harry, who had once hunted with Capstick, said that the writer was more or less correct. A wounded leopard is the most dangerous game. Harry was convinced that that's what they had on their hands, or convinced enough to go into the forest looking for blood.

They would go in Jason Stone's small pickup. No one with any sense would drive an open vehicle into thick cover if there was a chance of encountering a wounded leopard. With Karim, Jason, and the trackers standing in the back, there was no room for Stuart and me. In the event of a charge, Harry said, we would only be in the way, endangering ourselves and others. So we watched as the pickup forged its way through a stand of long grass and disappeared into the forest.

I settled beneath a sausage tree and listened for new bird songs, but most of what I was hearing now was familiar. The green phallic fruits, some up to two feet long, grew abundantly, hanging from the tree by long, thin stems, and the ground was littered with them. I picked one up. It was heavy enough to kill a man if it should fall on his head. Indeed, we had already heard stories of such fatalities. I wasn't sure that I believed them, but I moved out from beneath the canopy. I had also read that the fruit of the sausage tree is used by the native people to treat skin disorders, including cancer, but when I'd asked Demetrius about its uses he had laughed as though embarrassed by the question. Karim explained later that local tribesmen believe that a father can determine the size that an infant son's penis will assume in adulthood by some ritual involving the fruit.

It occurred to Stuart that the arrow, if we could find it, might show whether or not Steve had hit the leopard. While he stood at the rib cage where the leopard had crouched, I went inside the hut to the window through which Steve had shot. By assuming that the arrow had passed over the back of the cat, we determined not only a direction but a trajectory as well. According to our calculations, the arrow flew into the long grass, which seemed almost impenetrable to a man, but it must have struck the ground a few feet inside the thicket. As we were discussing these things, an old man who had been hanging around the edges of the clearing beat his way into the grass, trampled out a spot, leaned over, and picked up the shaft. It showed no trace of blood, though it could have been brushed clean by its passage through the grass.

The hunters returned two hours later. No leopard, no spoor.

THE MORNING was heating up. We bounced over the rough track that led through combretum thickets to the second bait tree. We were all hoping to find sign of a mature lion. Things were not going well for Steve. The absence of hippo in the pool had forced him to take an animal from the river with a rifle. He had missed a zebra with the bow and had to resort again to a firearm, which he had shot poorly. Yesterday afternoon he and Harry had stalked a record-book bushbuck, but it had escaped into the national park, and Steve was still smarting from the failure at the leopard blind. The only good bow shot he had made thus far had killed a wretched baboon. Yet, in spite of so many disappointments, he had not lost his composure, nor had I heard him grumble even once. He accepted responsibility for his mistakes, refusing to blame Harry or the trackers or the wind. Under similar circumstances I would not have behaved so well.

Harry stopped. Stretching before us, perhaps two hundred yards away, lay the marshy green meadow that contained at the far corner the hippo pool. Showing above the grass were the black backs of buffalo, moving from left to right. I raised my binoculars and caught a whiff of cattle, a rich stockyard smell. The herd was filling the meadow, more and more animals ambling in from the left. Oxpeckers rode their backs and flanks, and the big bulls swung their heads.

The seven of us in the vehicle were electrified by a current that arced from man to man. No one spoke. You could tell by the smell that the wind was in our favor. Harry stepped out, drawing his .458 Winchester magnum from its case. Karim handed Steve a bow as he buckled on his quiver. Stuart climbed down with the video camera, and Silas kicked off his flip-flops.

I wanted badly to go with the hunters, not out of reckless indifference to danger but to experience the sensation of being on the ground in the presence of buffalo. The one note common to every account of buffalo hunting I had read was the adrenaline rush that comes with stalking a bull. I wanted to see how afraid I would be.

But I knew better than to ask. Harry was taking Steve, Stuart, and Silas on foot to within bowshot of a hundred animals. Each person in addition to himself was his responsibility. Karim and I settled back on the high seat to watch.

The hunting party moved off to the right, crouched low, and soon disappeared through a hedge of brush. Harry's intention was to out-flank the slow-moving herd and get in position to pick out a trophy bull as they grazed past.

I asked Karim if he saw any good ones. He pointed out three or four—the ones with heavy bosses, he explained, old bulls whose horns met and merged in the middle of their foreheads. Where that was the case, the horns dropped in deep, sweeping curves before turning up into the sharp points that can easily impale a man.

"Tell me about your grandfather," I asked. The man I was referring to was actually Harry's grandfather, Porter Chapman from Canada, removed from Karim by another generation, but Karim knew who I meant. I had heard that Chapman was killed by a buffalo. This seemed to be a good time to get the details.

Of Porter Chapman's origins, his descendants knew only that he had come to Africa from Canada—some said Alberta, some said Toronto—in 1906 as a twenty-six-year-old butterfly collector for a French museum and settled along the Zambezi River. He soon abandoned butterflies in favor of elephants and began to make his living as an ivory hunter. In his middle years he married a woman of the Lozi tribe. She bore him four sons, the second of whom was Harry's father, Denis. By then he was cropping problem animals for the colonial government. One day in 1935, when he was fifty-five years old, he was notified of a buffalo that was terrorizing a village. Having injured a hoof in a wire snare, the animal was in an evil mood, keeping women from the fields and children from play. Thinking that this would be an easy and relatively safe assignment, Porter took his two older sons, fifteen-year-old Jack and thirteen-year-old Denis, so that they might begin their apprenticeship in hunting.

THE MEADOW before us was now filled with buffalo. The green grass reached the withers of the animals so that we could see only their black backs and, when they raised their heads, their horns. White cattle egrets flew up above the herd then settled back down on the wide, dusty shoulders. The animals moved steadily to the right, in the direction taken by the hunters. Karim thought that the lioness and grown cubs that we had seen in this place the other day might be pushing the herd, waiting to pick off a trailing calf.

THE HUNTERS meanwhile had slipped down into the bed of a sand river that provided cover as they worked their way out ahead of the herd. We could not see them, but they must have had time by now to get in position.

WHEN PORTER and his sons arrived at the village, Karim continued, the people grew excited. Here was a white man with a gun, come to rid them of their scourge. They led him out to the fields and showed him the thicket where the old bull was hiding, then retreated to the safety of their huts. Porter had his sons flanking him on either side, a few steps behind him. His approach to the thicket led him past a clump of brush, and from there the buffalo charged. The older boy, Jack, fled, the bull in his tracks. Porter could not shoot for fear of hitting his son, but he took off in pursuit. When the bull was breathing

down Jack's neck, the boy darted to the side, taking cover behind a tree, but his father did not see that and continued in pursuit. The bull suddenly wheeled, striking Porter in the groin with its horn and lifting him from the ground.

Karim did not know what became of the buffalo, but he did say that his great-grandfather lived long enough to instruct his sons in the care of their mother and the management of his estate. Then he entered into family lore.

As Karim was telling his story, Steve and Harry were lying against the bank of the sand river, surveying the herd. The animals were still too far out for a bow shot, but Harry wanted to find the best trophy.

From our position in the Land Cruiser, two or three hundred yards away from the hunters, we observed a bull detach himself from the herd and enter into the cavelike space beneath the overhanging branches of a combretum bush. Trying to rid himself of tick birds, Karim explained. The small birds eat the ticks and insects they find on large mammals. I had seen them on hippo, giraffe, and zebra, but buffalo are apparently their favorite source of food. Frequently, they serve the interests of their host by alerting it to approaching danger with their alarm notes, but sometimes they become pests. If in removing a tick they break the skin of the buffalo they may peck the wound bloody, causing irritation. The bull beneath the combretum bush was vigorously brushing his back against the thorny branches. Karim admired the width of his horns.

That very bush stood no more than thirty yards from the bank where the hunters lay. Harry saw it shaking, and then the bull stepped from behind it into their full view. The boss of its horns was deeply pitted and furrowed, and its gray scaly flanks looked like the skin of a black dog with mange. Steve drew his bow. The bull turned back to the bush and its head disappeared amidst foliage, but Harry had appraised the horns. He nodded. Steve rose to his feet and released the arrow. It struck the bull in the ribs, just back of the shoulder—higher than Steve would have liked, but he was convinced that the shot would prove fatal. As the bull wheeled and ran, it alarmed the herd, which began to lumber in the direction from which they had come.

Karim and I watched the stampede as it slowly gathered momentum, the black backs rocking heavily through the long grass. Then as one the herd swung about and pulled up, facing their tormentors. They were not facing us, but I was reminded of a statement by Robert Ruark: "A buffalo looks at you as though you owe him something." Yes, like your life. I was at the same time both safe in the vehicle and on the ground with the hunters, beneath a hundred frowns of consternation.

The wounded bull stood, backed up by the herd, its face a mask of black malevolence. Harry said to Steve, "Better let me finish him." Steve hardly had time to nod his consent when the big .458 roared.

Karim and I heard the shot and saw the stampede, but we were not able to pick out the wounded animal.

Another shot rang out, followed by a bellow. "That one hit him hard," Karim said.

The herd swung toward us. Karim removed the .355 H & H from its case. I aimed the Canon and began snapping pictures. Here they came. We were in no danger as long as we remained in the Land Cruiser, but it would be interesting to see how close the buffalo came to the vehicle.

Not as close as we had thought they might. The herd raised a great cloud of dust no more than fifty yards to our left as their hooves hammered the hard clay. In their wake stumbled an old bull. He went to his knees, staggered back onto his feet, and lurched forward.

I could see the hunters now, up ahead and a little off to the right, where the road ran alongside the meadow. Harry was waving his arms vigorously. "I think they're trying to get our attention," I told Karim.

He leapt into the driver's seat like a delinquent schoolboy caught at play when he should have been studying and fired up the engine. I slid in beside him. When we reached the hunting party, Harry climbed up the side onto the bench seat without speaking, but

Steve told me that they had been trying to get our attention from the time Harry shot. It was the first time Steve had heard Harry use profanity.

The bull was down just off the track up ahead. As we approached, it bellowed and tried to get to its feet, then collapsed. Within twenty steps of the animal Karim stopped. "Better hit him again," Harry said. "Break his back."

The blast of the rifle directly above my head knocked me over against Karim and deafened my left ear, but I had no one to blame but myself. Everyone else had heard Harry tell Steve to shoot and had stuck their fingers in their ears. I had been intent on the bull.

With the shot the bull groaned and lifted its head and forequarters, struggling mightily to get to its feet.

"Man, they take a lot of killing," Steve said.

"Again," Harry said.

This time I paid attention.

The whack of the bullet raised a little puff of dust. The bull did not react but lay as motionless as the stone it resembled.

"Once more."

"Isn't he dead now?"

"That's when they kill you."

Just then the bull lifted its muzzle an inch or two from the dust and from the deepest reach of its bovine soul emitted a long drawn out sigh, a moan that originated in the wellsprings of its vitality and resonated out through all its pipes like the note of an organ, and the animal released its life. None of us said anything. After a moment Harry walked over to the carcass and, still careful, leaned forward and gently touched the glazed eye with the muzzle of his rifle. Only then did congratulations begin.

FOR THE SAKE of good trophy photographs, the trackers nudge and push the animal into a photogenic position—not an easy task when it weighs two thousand pounds—and with their hand axes they chop away any grass that might stand between the camera and its subject. Stuart caught the procedure on video, I shot half a roll of film. After the picture taking, we drove on to the lion bait, leaving Demetrius and Silas to handle the carcass.

On the way Karim opened the cooler and passed out soft drinks and sandwiches. Expecting guinea fowl, which we had had almost every day, I was surprised by the fishy taste of sardine. I chased it with Coke and then decided that I was hungry enough to continue. Harry stopped at the bait, now little more than an empty cowl of hippo hide, but found no sign of a maned lion. Circling the tree, we passed downwind of the bait, and the effluvium flavored my taste of sardine. I choked it back, but when we drove up to the buffalo carcass I tossed what was left of the sandwich into the bush. Demetrius and Silas had hacked the buffalo in two, chopping it with their hand axes around the diaphragm as neatly as if they had used a chainsaw. Off to the side they had piled the partly digested contents of the rumens and intestines. I was impressed by the volume.

The odor here was not that of decay but of abdominal gases. I was eager for Harry to drive on, but Steve wanted to determine the location and the penetration of his arrow. He all but stuck his head and shoulders into the cavity of the chest and felt about the walls of the thorax with the palms of his hands. The shaft of the arrow had broken off during the bull's final run, but Steve found the hole it had made and put his finger through it. The broadhead had struck lung; the bull would have bled to death.

"Yes," said Harry, "but we would have been tracking him for the rest of the day."

He said nothing about the danger of such an enterprise, but we all understood.

Later I asked Steve what had happened to the broadhead. "I 'spect it ended up in somebody's pocket," he said.

▼▼▼

HARRY AND STEVE AND STUART departed for the skinning hut as soon as they finished supper, leaving Karim and me to spend an hour by the coals of the fire. The waxing moon had just risen, shedding a chilly light in the clear night sky, and hippos grunted from the river.

I offered Karim a cigar but he declined. He had been in bed all day with malaria and was still not feeling well.

I wondered how he would do as a professional hunter. He seemed capable of repairing any kind of broken machine; he knew firearms, ammo, and ballistics; and he had the eye of an eagle, able to spot game from a moving vehicle at great distances. But he lacked Harry's authoritative manner. He had a sweet spirit.

"Is Harry a naturally reserved person," I asked, "or is that just his professional demeanor?"

Karim smiled, a shy but engaging flash of perfectly even white teeth. "That is Harry's true nature," he said. "But when you get to know him, he is very approachable. He tends to be quiet because he does not want to be perceived as a man who talks too much."

"The two of you grew up together?"

"Harry's father owns a farm on the upper Zambezi. Harry spent much time there as a boy and then went off to boarding school in Lusaka. I didn't really get to know him well until we were older."

"So it wasn't Harry who got you started hunting?"

"No, it was my father."

Karim fell silent. After a while he said, "We lost him two years ago."

"I'm sorry."

"He was taken by a crocodile."

"Oh, Karim. How terrible."

"Yes," he said. "It was terrible."

He paused again. "He was fishing in the Zambezi River. He had bought a farm on the river several years before, and he went fishing almost every afternoon. He knew better than to get close to the water. He just got careless."

Karim spoke softly. I could barely hear him, and I could not see his face in the dark, but he was saying things that I could not ask him to repeat. "No one knows exactly how it happened. Some of the men who worked for my father were downstream a little distance, but he was by himself. They heard a cry, they said, but by the time they reached the place where he had been he was gone. He must have been very close to the edge. He may have been landing a fish. Crocs are very quick."

I was reminded of how we had laughed at Harry's story of the crocs taking baboons from the roots of a tree. Had Karim been at the table when Harry imitated the squeal of the victims? I could not remember, but I thought surely not.

"They saw bubbles on the water, and a couple of them went out in a canoe and felt around underwater with a pole but they did not find anything. The croc must have taken him out to the main channel."

"What was your father's name?" I asked.

"Karim Abdul Hassan."

I let the syllables hang in the night, glad to have given the son the opportunity to speak his father's name.

HARRY'S FATHER Denis and his uncle Frank, sons of Porter Chapman and a woman of mixed race, both married women of color. Denis's wife, Eva, was of Lozi and English-Jewish blood, and Frank's wife was Roman Catholic. Their daughter Juliet, Karim's mother, married Karim Abdul Hassan, descendant of Arab slave traders. Harry's wife, Layla, was a Lozi, and Karim had married a woman of German descent who professed Christianity. From such an ethnic and religious brew, I wondered how Karim had figured out who he was. In any case, he seemed to know.

He asked about the books I had written and if I was planning to write about the safari.

"I have wanted to, but I don't think I know enough."

"Then you must come back and stay longer. Three weeks is too short a time."

"I don't see how I can keep from coming back, but writing a book is not so much a matter of the time you spend in a place as what you do with it. Steve has already learned things, by hunting, that I won't get to, but I'm not here just to write a report on Steve's activities. In other words, for me to write a book worth reading—I mean, the kind of book that I would want to read—something will have to happen. I will have to find myself in a story. Like the stories y'all tell."

Karim smiled. "Anything can happen in Africa, but you'll need to live to tell about it."

I laughed because I thought I was expected to. "Right," I said, "but the best stories are the ones with blood in them, I don't know why."

"Maybe it's because that's what people do. Animals too. They bleed. Muslims believe that the life of the animal is in the blood. That's why we cut the throat."

I was reminded of the old hymn, "Power in the Blood," and the idea arced the gap. Karim asked, "Are you a Christian?"

What a naked question. Asked in the light of a camp fire, against a background of hippo sounds, it required a naked answer—no equivocation, no academic window dressing—yet what would a simple yes or no mean to this young Muslim from Zambia who had lost his father to a crocodile? Did he understand Christianity as a cultural bias mediated by the historical church or as an active faith grounded in scripture and experience? "Consider the difference between Steve and me on this safari," I said at last. "Steve is the hunter, I the observer. Most people who call themselves Christian can probably be divided into two such groups. The observer goes to church, recites the creed, even takes communion, but whatever happens, happens only in his head. On one occasion Jesus asked his disciples, 'Who do men say that I am?' The 'observer Christian' can answer that question all day long because it's just academic, see? But then Jesus asked them, 'Who do you say that I am?' And that's where the observer runs out of answers. In fact, he will usually object to the question as none of your business, and that's a pretty good sign that he's just an observer. The hunter kind of Christian, on the other hand, has a story to tell because he's in pursuit of something real, not just a theological idea."

"And that's the kind you are, the hunter?"

"I would like to think so. But there are hunters and then there are hunters, as you know."

Karim did not respond. We sat without speaking in the loud African night. Then he asked, "Which translation of the Bible do you use? Christians seem to have so many."

"I like the King James."

"Why is that?"

"Because it contains the finest English ever written. Listen: *The*

Lord is my shepherd; I shall not want. He maketh me to lie down in green pastures; he leadeth me beside the still waters. He restoreth my soul; he leadeth me in the paths of righteousness for his name's sake. Whenever God speaks in English, I suspect that's the way he sounds."

"Yea, though I walk through the valley of the shadow of death," Karim recited, "I will fear no evil: for thou art with me; thy rod and thy staff they comfort me."

"Ah," I said.

We finished the psalm together, Karim's quiet Zambian English blending with my southern pronunciation:

"And I will dwell in the house of the Lord forever."

When we had ended, we both remained silent, listening to the hippos. After a minute Karim stood up. We shook hands.

"If Steve gets the leopard," I said, "be sure to wake me up."

▼ ▼ ▼

I WAS IN DEEP SLEEP when the light came on in my room—a sense of unreality, not knowing what time it was, still in my dream, and Karim standing at my bed: "Wake up, Doc. Doc. Wake up. They got the leopard."

At the word "leopard" I bolted into full consciousness. I heard a commotion outside, the chanting of many voices. I tore the mosquito netting from beneath my mattress and stumbled into my clothes. From the doorway I could see the Land Cruiser approaching the gate of the camp, headlights flashing. The occupants were singing, their voices coming into the camp before them.

The safari staff were standing in a line beside the dining hut, clapping and singing, joining their voices to the chanting of the men in the vehicle.

> Ba Stevi, na lebo ba wina chipolopolo,
> Eyee', chipolopolo,
> Kaingo, eyee', chipolopolo.

The vehicle pulled up and the people gathered at the back, still chanting and stamping the bare dirt with bare feet. Steve climbed down. A white chair of molded plastic was handed through the crowd. Steve was seated in it, then hoisted shoulder-high and shuffled around in a circle, followed by the train of celebrants.

Eyee', chipolopolo,
Kaingo, eyee', chipolopolo.

One clear voice rang out, leading the chorus, and the African darkness refrained, *chipolopolo.*

In spite of the plastic chair and the swinging beams of flashlights, the moment was at once both primal and timeless. Kaingo, the old marauder who slinks among village huts at night, even now, sometimes stealing children—that ancient nightmare was vanquished. Bwana Stevi had won by the bullet and all were glad.

Except Bwana Stevi himself. From his exalted seat he looked down upon the celebration, bemused but not elated. When the chair was lowered to the ground and the chanting ceased, people gathered at the back of the Land Cruiser to admire the cat, but Steve came over to me. "I guess you figured out who shot the leopard."

The first streaks of daylight were showing through the trees. Steve and I walked over to the fire circle and sat down. Against a saffron light geese and storks were flying the river.

The leopard had come to the bait. Harry and Steve, both awake, had been alerted by the crunching of bone. The sky was just starting to pale, but it was still too dark to see an animal on the ground. Harry switched on the flood. The leopard was crouched at the rib cage of the zebra, its head and shoulders hidden by the carcass. Steve held his aim as far forward as possible and released the arrow, striking the cat through the ribs. It sprang into the air with a yowl and bolted into the darkness. "I got him," Steve said quietly to Harry.

"But a little far back," Harry said.

"Give him time."

Harry swung the powerful beam against the dark wall of vegetation, and, lo, the eyes of the leopard—burning coals. He was crouched against long grass. Harry brought the rifle to his shoulder. "Better let me finish him."

"He's not going anywhere," Steve said. "Just let him lay down and bleed out."

"We can't risk it," Harry said.

"It was just like the buffalo," Steve told me. "Harry doesn't want to go into the bush after a wounded animal."

"After that lion last year, I can understand why, can't you?"

Steve didn't respond. We walked in silence. "I'll tell you what I think happened, Doc. We both assumed that the leopard we saw after I shot was the one I had just hit. So when Harry asked me to let him shoot it, he thought he was just finishing off a wounded animal. But when we went over and examined it, the only other wound we found was in its foot, and Harry thinks that that's where the arrow hit."

"And you don't?"

"Let's go take a look."

We walked over to the Land Cruiser. Everyone had departed to whatever they had to do. The leopard lay in the back, on its belly, its chin propped on a yellow plastic can of coolant. I reached out to touch the spotted coat, to stroke against the grain the thick nap of its hair, but that close the odor made me gag. Not even the night I'd spent in the skinning hut had prepared me for the foul reek of this gorgeous creature. It was a stench of putrefaction folded in with the smell of cat, as though the leopard after mating had rolled in carrion. But the odor didn't bother Steve. He lifted the left front paw. Sure enough, there was a small hole through the top of it. "Harry thinks that the leopard jumped at the sound of the bowstring and the arrow got him in the foot, but this isn't an arrow wound. This wound came from fighting. Maybe even a baboon."

"So you don't think Harry knows?"

"I think it was an honest mistake, but he can't afford to admit it."

"But you got a leopard with your bow, Steve. Nothing can change that."

"I don't know."

As WE RODE OUT to check lion baits, the stench of the leopard seemed to follow us, as though the back of the Land Cruiser, the space directly below and behind me, had not been washed out, though I knew it had been. Yet the odor, or the memory of it in my nostrils, evoked the splendor of the leopard's coat. Black spots on an orange ground doesn't begin to describe the play of light upon that pelage. Again and again, in trying to impart a sense of the presence of a large animal I have been tempted to say that it seemed to glow with a light from within. After seeing the leopard dead in the morning sun I knew I would never use that phrase to describe any other creature. Of the animals I have seen in the wild, none truly burned like the carcass of that cat.

▼ ▼ ▼

UNLIKE SOME PROFESSIONAL HUNTERS, Harry tolerated cameras—Stuart's video and my Canon—but I had learned right away that on this safari hunting took precedence over photography. If we came upon a good photo op, Harry might stop, but he was being paid to find game for Steve. Even so, I had gotten what I hoped were sharply focused close-ups of elephants and giraffes. By the end of the first week I was beginning to believe in the possibility of a decent portfolio of African animals.

At some point along the torturous eleven-mile stretch of broken black cotton soil, Karim said, "Kudu," and pointed out into the combretum fields. Harry stopped. He and Steve conferred for a moment and then Harry turned to me. "Want a shot at that kudu, Doc?"

He meant with a camera, of course, not a rifle. I climbed down and attached the monopod. Kudu are more wary than most plains game. Their hearing is exceptionally keen, and their eyes and nose are almost as good. In this open country with nothing but scattered combretum bushes for cover, Steve would have had a hard time stalking to within bow range, but my telephoto lens might just be long enough.

Harry led me along a game trail through short grass and jumbled clods, the path pocked with the deep, hardened molds of elephant, buffalo, and hippo tracks. I wanted to impress Harry by walking silently over the rough ground, but the soles of my boots kept scraping against the bricklike earth. Harry halted, bent low, as intense as if

I had been armed with a rifle. "The way to stalk, Doc," he whispered, "is to walk easy. You're trying too hard to be quiet."

The kudu were on the far side of a large combretum. The breeze was in our favor. Under cover of the bush we made our approach, flushing a flock of brilliant green lovebirds. Harry stopped, his hand extended in a signal to freeze. Two large brown female kudu moved out from behind the bush, unaware of us but quartering away to the left. "Get ready," Harry whispered.

I checked the camera settings and prepared for a shot, but the bull, which often follows his harem, did not appear. "He's still there," Harry said. We eased to the right of the bush, and he was there all right but 150 yards out. He had walked straight away, keeping the bush between us. I set the monopod and extended the lens, my heart pounding. He was standing still, tall and dark gray against the tawny grass, his majestic head raised, and his horns—two and half twists—spiraled like branches of a tree. I snapped and snapped.

Well within rifle range, I thought, but to get the picture I wanted I would have to sneak to within a bow shot. Not even Harry was going to get that close to a kudu. Yet I returned to the vehicle exhilarated. With Harry's help I had stalked African game. Whether the film would show a trophy I would have to wait and see, but for an observer I had almost hunted. I had been on the ground in Africa. That night I wrote in my journal, "Today I had an opportunity to stalk a kudu bull with the camera, guided by Harry—an experience as close to hunting African big game as I will ever have. Or want." At the time I made that entry, I really believed it.

Part Three

KUDU

I got a fine male kudu. We have no grain and live on meat alone. . . . The
kudu stood five feet six inches high; horns, three feet on the straight.
DAVID LIVINGSTONE, *The Last Journals*, December 19, 1866

"Inches don't mean anything," Pop said. "They're
damned wonderful kudu."
ERNEST HEMINGWAY, *Green Hills of Africa*

I did not mind killing anything, any animal, if I killed it cleanly, they all
had to die and my interference with the nightly and the seasonal killing
that went on all the time was very minute and I had
no guilty feeling at all.
ERNEST HEMINGWAY, *Green Hills of Africa*

I cannot understand why I itch so much to use the gun in the rack behind
me. My camera will not do. I need to kill only one animal and then be
done with it forever (at least that is what I tell myself).
JOHN HEMINWAY, *No Man's Land*

V

▼▼▼▼▼

In December of 1855, on the lower Kafue River in what is now Zambia, David Livingstone stood at the top of a bluff looking out on a wide green valley. The plain below was filled with more large animals than he had seen anywhere in Africa. Hundreds of buffaloes and zebras grazed in the open spaces, and "lordly elephants" fanned their ears and waved their trunks. He wished for a camera. "Such scenes," he would write, "are destined, as guns increase, to pass away from the earth." He and his party descended to the plain and walked among the animals without alarming them. They were remarkably tame.

Two months later Livingstone was sitting in the shade of a great mahogany tree not far from the Zambezi River, contemplating the carcass of an elephant his men had killed that morning. It lay downhill from where he sat, a good distance away, but he could hear the steady drone of blowflies that swarmed in a dark cloud above the clay-colored mound. The elephant's belly was distended, its legs stiffened, its flank caked dark with blood. He didn't blame the men. They had been subsisting for a fortnight on coarse millet, and all of them, himself included, were suffering the effects of the meager diet. When they had spied the elephant, an old bull with one good tusk, they had dropped their loads on the spot and taken off with their spears in wild pursuit. The killing had been a prolonged butchery, covering more than a mile of ground and accompanied by shouts of warning, cries of encouragement, and grunts of satisfaction. Toward the end, as the bull swayed upon its tree-trunk legs, its shoulders and sides bristling with spears, one man dashed up behind it and axed its hamstrings. The bull's hindquarters buckled. Waving its trunk, it settled onto its side.

Livingstone insisted that he never enjoyed hunting, much less the killing, but he shot animals when he needed to. If he and his men were starving, as they often were, he would shoot with as little hesitation, he said, "as I should cut off a patient's leg." What troubled him about this kill was the mad delight the porters had taken in the slaughter, the savagery of their dancing and whooping around the noble beast as it lay twitching. The commotion of the killing had attracted a passing band of Banyai, elephant hunters themselves, and they too had been appalled by the behavior of Livingstone's men. One of the Banyai had emptied his snuff box upon the roots of a tree—a gesture Livingstone found curious until the man explained. "I see you are travelling with people who don't know how to pray: I therefore offered the only thing I had in their behalf, and the elephant soon fell." When the elephant at last lay dead, Livingstone had approached the whooping mob dancing around the carcass, and one of his porters said, as though in self-defense, "God gave it to us. He said to the old beast, 'Go up there: men are come who will kill and eat you.'"

As Livingstone sat by the bloated carcass, waiting for his men to return from the paramount chief to whom he had sent them for permission to begin the butchering, he turned his attention to insects "as tiny as grains of sand" that were crawling about on nearby boxes. Examining several colorful new species through a magnifying glass, he remarked that it was strange that men should abhor them. Then like a bolt it struck him: elephants and other large animals abhor us. "We are the horrid biped," he would write, "that ruins their peace."

Livingstone explained his lack of interest in hunting by saying that he had "but little of the hunting-*furore* in my composition." Maybe, but he had some. Just before he witnessed the beauty of the Kafue plains, he had killed an elephant himself. He had set out in search of buffalo and had shot a bull, hitting it three times without bringing it down. When the wounded animal turned to charge, Livingstone and his men fled to an outcropping of rocks. In the process they surprised an elephant. Despairing of the buffalo, the missionary shot at it, striking it in the front leg. Eventually, his men brought it to a stand

and Livingstone put a shot in the brain. The next day, as the men were cutting up the elephant, a nearby village gathered to enjoy the feast. Livingstone was pleased by their delight in so much meat.

During the festivities he noticed at a distance of two miles a cow elephant with her calf. Livingstone took out his telescope. The calf was rolling playfully in a mudhole while its mother stood by, keeping watch. To his dismay he spied a line of his porters stalking the elephants.

The account of the event in *Missionary Travels* drips with Victorian sentimentality. Even Dickens could not have drawn a more heartbreaking picture of a valiant mother defending her child.

Livingstone sent runners to stop the killing of the calf but they arrived too late. The cow, with dozens of spears sticking in her body, turned on the men in her grief and rage, but they were too many for her. Livingstone writes,

> I turned from the spectacle of the destruction of noble animals, which might be made so useful in Africa, with a feeling of sickness; and it was not relieved by the recollection that the ivory was mine, though that was the case. I regretted to see them killed, and more especially the young one, the meat not being at all necessary at that time; but it is right to add that I did not feel sick when my own blood was up the day before. We ought, perhaps, to judge those deeds more leniently in which we ourselves have no temptation to engage. Had I not been previously guilty of doing the very same thing, I might have prided myself on superior humanity when I experienced the nausea in viewing my men kill these two.

VI

▼▼▼▼▼

IN THE VESTIBULE of the chalet was a low bamboo shelf upon which sat a basin of water. Above the basin hung a mirror. After an early breakfast I was standing at the shelf brushing my teeth, preparing for another day of rough riding through the bush. In the early light my face in the glass was dark. I was getting sun, maybe too much. I found the sunscreen in my shaving kit. Steve came walking up. "You think you could come up with two thousand dollars if you had to?"

I thought he was about to propose that we charter a plane to another camp. He wanted to hunt lechwe and had mentioned the possibility a time or two. I would have liked to see new country but not for that amount of money. "If I had to, I guess. Why?"

"That's what it will cost you to shoot a kudu. Trophy fee and taxidermy. If you want to."

Gosh.

My first impulse was to say no and not because of the money. The old fever—the "hunting furore"—that had once kept me awake all night before opening day of deer season had long since abated. The change had begun at about the time I was diagnosed with cancer, causing me to wonder at first if my growing sense of mortality had bred in me a greater sympathy for other creatures. But I had decided not. To think so was just a way of ennobling an ordinary, perhaps inevitable development. The truth was that with success and familiarity hunting had become a little boring. At the same time, surgery, radiation, and more recently hormone therapy, which blocks the body's production of testosterone, had drained me of energy. An old man once said to Isak Dinesen, "The person who can take delight in a sweet tune without wanting to learn it, in a beautiful woman without wanting to possess her, or in a magnificent head of game without wanting to shoot it, has not got a human heart." I felt that my heart was still in pretty good shape, but I no longer felt a rage to own. If that indifference had diminished my humanity, it had also set me free from a certain restlessness, and I was enjoying the peace—perhaps another way of understanding the difference between observer and hunter.

But a kudu. A magnificent head, sure enough, and a subject worthy of Hemingway's craft.

It crossed my mind that I had no wall space for a mounted head that size, and even if I did, what place would such a thing have in my home? It would utterly alter any room in which it hung.

But it was not the head I wanted. It was the hunt, intimate contact, the mystery of blood, the colors of Africa.

"Yes," I said. "Yes."

THE FIRST THING we did that morning was practice marksmanship. I had not shot a rifle in a long time. I had never shot a .300 Weatherby magnum. Harry pulled up at the edge of the zebra plain, got out and set up the shooting tripod. The trackers paced off a hundred yards and with a hand ax hacked out on the trunk of a tree a target the size of a playing card. The morning was still chilly, but I removed my jacket, uncomfortably conscious of the eyes of six men.

I was touched by Steve's generosity. Two years earlier, hunting in South Africa, he had taken a very good kudu with his bow from a blind, but because of the different circumstances on this safari, his best chance at another would require a rifle, and he did not want to do that. Still, a kudu is a great prize. He didn't have to offer it to me.

I held the crosshairs on the blaze and squeezed the trigger. Demetrius, who had been standing to the side, went over and examined the shot. An inch or two off to the right. Close enough.

A LION for Steve still took priority, but a kudu might appear at any moment. From now on, I would be on call. The opportunity to hunt altered my perception of the familiar landscape—the light and wind and temperature, the terrain and vegetation, even my position in the vehicle. It was not that I was more aware of these elements than I had been, but I was differently aware. Knowing that I was now a hunter, that the spotting of a kudu would put a rifle in my hands, effected a kind of metaphysical change. I was consequential in a way that I had not been yesterday. I felt weighty with responsibility, not just to stalk quietly and to shoot well, should that opportunity occur, but to understand what I was doing and to talk and act accordingly.

THE ROUGH eleven-mile track through the combretum plain followed a sand river that was the boundary of the national park. I had begun to think of that run as "Kudu Alley," though we saw as many puku and eland among the orchardlike scattering of bushes. As we were driving toward the third lion bait, lurching and jouncing across broken ground, we came upon a stagnant pool in the river bed, and, lounging in the pool, like a fat man in a bathtub, a hippo. We got out for a closer look. Though hippos are dangerous, the bank on our side was too steep for him to climb. He tried to immerse himself but the muddy water proved too shallow. He wallowed down as deep as he could, but his broad back remained exposed, and his tiny periscopic eyes. His hide was scored by two pink gouges.

"That's a sick hippo," Harry said. "He's been driven away from the herd by a larger bull."

"I wish we had found him the other day," Steve said. "That's an easy bow shot."

"Too bad," Harry said. "And he's going to die anyway if he doesn't get back to the river tonight, which is a long trip."

I moved to the edge of the bank for a closer shot with the Canon. The trackers were tossing dirt clods at the miserable animal, trying to provoke a reaction. It worked. Suddenly, the hippo rose surging from the pool, flinging mud and water. The massive head looked like something molded in clay by a child. The huge mouth opened, showing tusks, and the hippo bellowed in its rage. The trackers laughed. As though maddened by their contempt, the hippo lumbered up onto the low, sloping ground of the opposite bank and swung around to our side. I was witnessing the action through the lens of my camera, which framed and distanced the creature into a kind of television unreality, but when it came toward us, I was surprised by the speed and agility of its stumpy legs—"turtle legs," Teddy Roosevelt called them.

"Get to the car," Harry said. "Quick."

No one argued.

Safely seated in the Land Cruiser, Stuart said, "It's hard to believe that he could have outrun us."

"He has two more legs than you do," Harry said.

I asked Karim what hippos are called in Nyanja.

"Mvuu means hippos in general. Ndomondo refers to an individual bull in its . . . " Karim paused. "How would you say? In its hugeness."

"Then this hippo was ndomondo, right?"

Demetrius and Silas smiled at each other, and Karim nodded. "Right."

"Ndomondo," I repeated. "What a perfect name."

Though kudu are considered woodland antelope, the few we had seen had been browsing in the open combretum fields. The reason we were not finding them in the woods was obvious. In cover they are too well-camouflaged to be seen. With narrow, widely spaced chalk stripes on gray flanks, they can disappear by standing still.

Approaching the Milyoti Gate village on our way back to camp for

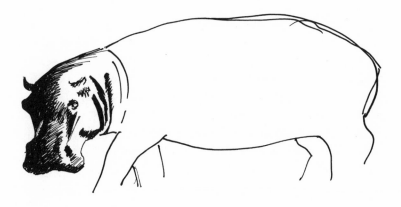

the evening, we entered a stand of scrubby trees, heavy cover on both sides of the road. Karim said, "Kudu," and I turned from reverie in time to see a large animal merging into shadow. Harry drove on another two hundred yards before pulling over. "Come on, Doc," he said. I climbed down the ladder fixed to the side of the vehicle and Karim handed me the rifle. Harry shook a little baby powder into the breeze. It drifted back toward him, and he moved into the woods. I followed, feeling unconnected. This was happening too suddenly. I was not prepared to hunt. Harry moved ahead quickly, crouched over, pausing now and then just long enough to scan openings, communicating by hand signals.

The setting sun was sending orange rays through the trees. A cooling breeze stirred the dry leaves, causing them to rattle. Not even Harry would be able to see a kudu in this flickering light and shadow. I became aware of a strange birdcall, high-pitched and drawn out, moving ahead of us as though it meant to show us the way to the kudu. Presently, Harry stopped and relaxed. The hunt was over.

"He's gone," he said. "The go-away bird told him we were coming."

Harry was referring to the gray lourie, infamous among hunters for alerting game by a cry that sounds to our ears remarkably similar to the words *go-awaaaay*. Apparently, it sounds the same to kudu and other animals. "They actually pay attention to the call?" I asked.

"Oh yes," Harry said. "The go-away bird is their friend."

It occurred to me that the call that had warned the kudu had sent us away as well.

WE DROPPED MBULUMA at the village and headed toward camp. It was getting dark fast. A mile from the compound we came upon a herd of elephants in thin acacia scrub just off the road. There were about a dozen of them—cows and calves of various ages—and they were moving in our direction. Harry drove on beyond them, then stopped, though he left the engine running. If they passed close enough, there might be enough light for photographs. Like elephants in a circus parade, they filed across the road forty yards behind us, immense and dark in the gloomy dusk, and the smell of them was strong in the chill air. I fiddled with the camera. Just as I was bringing it to my eye, a trumpet blast all but unseated me. Here came one of the old cows, ears flared and trunk raised. Harry floorboarded the gas pedal and the Land Cruiser leaped. In a minute or two the lights of camp appeared. "She wasn't serious," Harry said. "A serious elephant won't trumpet. She just wanted us out of there."

When the camp had gone to bed, I took my journal over to the dining hut. The fluorescent tube overhead created a square of cold white light within the grass walls. Hyenas yipped and laughed from the woods outside the fence, and an ill-tempered hippo complained from the river. I mixed a gin and tonic, hoping that the old remedy for malaria might bolster the effects of the prophylaxis I was taking, for mosquitoes were biting my ankles. Within the square of light I felt secure but blind to the world beyond the walls, for out there all was black. I walked over to the low front wall of the compound. The moon, which had been but a mere sliver just a few days before, had waxed now to half full. As my eyes adjusted to the darkness, the night grew brighter. The wide river beach shone pale in the moonlight, and the bare yard of the compound was stippled with moon shadows. As the shadows stirred and shifted, it was easy to imagine a leopard slipping through the camp.

I returned to the hut and opened the journal, but for the first time I felt that I had nothing to say. I could describe our little adventure with the hippo but it had come to nothing, as had the kudu alerted by the lourie and the elephant's mock charge. Each of those animals had told us in its own way to get the hell out of its yard.

▼ ▼ ▼

The next morning, as Harry turned onto the familiar track that would take us through the combretum plain, I scanned the alleys and openings among the scattered bushes. By "bush" I mean a plant twelve to fifteen feet high, just as wide, and shaggy with thorny, whip-like shoots that overhung the central portion to create a sort of umbrella, inside which both predator and prey or even a buffalo might escape the midday sun. Puku, impala, kudu, and eland browsed the leaves of these plants, but spotting them as we jounced and lurched along the rough track was a challenge. Until then I had left that responsibility to the eagle eyes of Karim and the trackers and concentrated on birds, but now I too was hunting. I wanted to be able to claim the whole experience, from the first sighting to the last photograph.

Puku were the most frequently seen, the burnished, deer-size antelope occurring usually in small harems of six or eight females and young followed by a herd buck. Steve had two puku on his license but so far had not seen a head impressive enough to take. When someone spotted a group, Harry would stop, scan the animals through binoculars, then shake his head. "Nanh."

Infrequently and at great distances we saw groups of eland. In the concession we were hunting, these largest of African antelopes were under protection by the game department that season, apparently because of reduced numbers, but Harry never failed to stop when one of the party spotted them, and we were always glad to spend a few minutes watching the large, stone-colored animals through binoculars.

We saw kudu more often, though they were not an animal we could count on, especially not a mature bull. Yet, where cows were present, it paid to search carefully for the old male.

Less than fifteen minutes into the eleven-mile run, a loose flock of carmine bee-eaters, hawking for insects in the clear light overhead, distracted my attention. I had counted twelve or fourteen when Stuart, seated next to me, said, "Elephants." A scattered herd, just ahead and not far off the road, was feeding among the combretum. Harry stopped. I reached for my camera, but Karim whispered, "Kudu, Doc" and drew the .300 Weatherby from its case. My heart began to pound. Where the kudu was I had no idea but I had only to follow Harry. Steve handed me a fist full of cartridges and I opened the bolt. "Okay, Doc, it's your show."

Harry was standing in the game trail that would take us toward the antelope, looking anxious. The folded shooting sticks rested upon his shoulder like a fishing pole. Demetrius stood at his side, carrying the big rifle, and Karim fell in behind me, armed with a .458. If this had been a camera stalk, I doubt we would have risked moving through the feeding elephants, but Harry proceeded confidently and I followed, glancing left and right. There's no way to appreciate fully the size of an elephant without walking on his ground in his presence. We were easing through the middle of a herd, elephants on both sides. They seemed untroubled by our intrusion and continued to feed, uprooting large bundles of dry grass and shaking the dirt from them before stuffing them into their mouths. But several paused and considered us. A half-grown calf moved closer to its mother's flank. None of the elephants had particularly impressive tusks, but the sculpted skulls in the glare of the sun, the weight of placidly swinging trunks, and the slowly moving ears made me forget for a moment that we were hunting kudu. Harry would tell me later that a charging elephant can often be turned by a shot fired in the air, but I didn't know that as we passed through the herd. The breeze was rich with their odor, and I was wide awake.

With the elephants behind us I remembered that what I was afraid of was screwing up the hunt, of spooking the kudu or, worst of all, wounding it by a poor shot. Climbing down from the observer's seat in the hunting car and stepping onto the dry, cracked ground with a rifle in my hand had altered the nature of reality.

Thorns scratched my bare knees and calves, and the sun baked my neck. Harry eased on ahead in a low crouch, moving quickly. I tried to remember exactly what he had said when we were stalking with the camera, about walking naturally, but the toes of my boots kept scraping clods. I was terribly afraid of his disapproval.

I could do a better job of this if I were by myself, I thought.

Harry's left hand, palm down, motioned for me to stop. He turned his head, pointed at my feet, then put his index finger to his lips. I nodded. The incessant calls of turtle doves—*pontalba, pontalba, pontalba*—only made the morning hotter. I was breathing hard, but whether from excitement or exertion I couldn't tell. I brushed sweat from my eyes with the sleeve of my shirt. Was this something I really wanted to do or had I just responded too quickly to the magic of the word *kudu*?

Harry was maneuvering so as to keep the combretum bushes between us and the kudu, and the breeze was in our face. I was having trouble keeping up and staying quiet at the same time. I focused on Harry's thin brown legs, the tight kinks of hair that lay flat against his skin, the dark scars of the puncture wounds from the lion. I don't know how far we walked. He stopped and I froze. He peeped around a brushy edge to the right, quickly set the shooting tripod, and urgently waved me forward. Something was happening on the left— two females moving away—but Harry was pointing to the right. I set the rifle on the support. The bull was at least 150 yards out, maybe 200, standing tall in the pale grass, looking back toward us, and his neck bulged. This was an exact repetition of the camera stalk of two days ago, brought about by an agency beyond my understanding. For all I knew, we were standing in the same spot, looking at the same bull. His dark spiraling horns rose from his head like a miracle. My hands were trembling and I could hardly catch my breath. Harry whispered, "Relax, Doc," but sweat stung my eyes.

"Think you can take him?" Harry asked.

"Yes."

With a deep breath I tried to hold the rifle steady, but the bull was so small in the scope that the crosshairs wavered back and forth from hindquarter to shoulder. It occurred to me in a flash that I had no business shooting this animal without knowing more about it. When was the time of rut, for example, or did bulls fight for their harems as elk do? I lifted my eye from the scope and took another breath, wiped sweat from my eyes. I regretted not knowing. A shoulder shot will break him down, I was thinking, just don't hit him in the gut, hold forward, better to miss altogether than to hit him in the gut. Far better.

At the report of the rifle the kudu trotted forward, apparently unscathed. I jacked in another bullet.

"Shoot again," Harry urged.

I did but with no more effect than before. The kudu bounded away toward distant cover.

"Ahh," Harry said. "You missed."

"You're sure?"

"I saw the bullet kick up dust. You shot in front of him."

"Was he the same one I photographed?"

Harry gave me a look. "Not unless he's grown a few more inches of horn in the past two days. This one was a dandy. But he'll still be there tomorrow."

As EARLY as the 1920s photographic safaris in Kenya were beginning to rival hunting in popularity. Isak Dinesen writes that photography "is a more refined sport than shooting, and provided you can make the lion join in the spirit of it you may here, at the end of a pleasant, platonic affair, without bloodshed on either side, blow one another a kiss and part like civilized beings. I have no real knowledge of the art; I was a fairly good shot with a rifle, but I cannot photograph."

That marvelous sexual analogy may be the best comparison to the difference between photography and hunting that I have ever read or heard, but she offers another that was closer to my recent experience. Even the best photographs of wild game, she says, bore less resemblance to the animals "than the chalk portraits drawn up on the kitchen door by our Native porters." What I learned that hot morning on the combretum plain is that photography is to hunting what photographs of cave paintings are to the actual paintings. Or so it seems, based on descriptions I have read of the decorated caves. When I stepped from the observer's seat in the hunting car, climbed down the ladder, and took the rifle, I entered into possibility such as no camera can record. The distance at which I shot proved too great in my excited condition, just as the photographed kudu had been too far out for a good, sharp picture, but after the hunt I returned to the vehicle with the feeling that I had experienced more of Africa.

▼ ▼ ▼

HARRY HAD SAID the kudu I missed would be there tomorrow. When the sun came up again, we set out in search of him. It was another glorious blue morning, crisp and tangy as it had been yesterday and every day since our arrival. The thermometer was as reliable as a clock—the mercury climbing with the hour until it peaked around 3:30—and the barometer was steady. We followed the same dim track across the combretum plain that we had taken every day, so that you had the feeling of running in place rather than marking progress in time, of dancing to a rhythm of day and night in which the calendar had no meaning. Each cycle of sunrise and sunset and each circle of the route took us more deeply into Africa. Only the waxing moon, rising later each night, reminded you that this would eventually end.

We traversed the area where I had made the stalk but spotted no kudu. To my surprise I found myself relieved. I tried at first to deny the feeling and pretend that I was disappointed, but it did no good. I was relieved and might as well admit it. Maybe I was afraid of missing another shot, especially under the eyes of an audience eager for my success, but there was more to it than that, and what it was was not hard to understand—I had not yet developed the mind of the hunter. My psyche was not right. I was willing to hunt but my soul was not yet attuned to it.

It didn't help that yesterday, an hour after I missed the kudu, young Stuart shot a record-book impala. Steve had offered him an opportunity to hunt impala for the same reason he offered me the kudu. So, while searching for kudu we had been keeping our eyes open for a good impala for Stuart. Just after my failure, Harry spied a lone buck in the combretum and pulled over. Stuart handed the video to Steve, who was a complete stranger to such technology, took the rifle from Karim, and the entourage set out, leaving me in the hunting car with silent Mbuluma. The hunters soon disappeared among the combretum. Mbuluma and I waited in the vehicle, in the full glare of the sun, he without a hat. After a long time there was a shot. I looked at Mbuluma. He nodded. I asked if he was sure. I didn't want Stuart to make a shot that would make me look worse than I already did. Something small in me was hoping that he'd missed. But Mbuluma clapped his hands together smartly to show that he had heard the thwack of the bullet.

Before long, Karim came walking up, his handsome dark face flashing a brilliant smile, his teeth perfectly white against his beard and mustache. He was holding his hands out from his head to indicate the width of the horns.

"How long a shot?" I asked.

"One sixty. Perfect shot."

A hundred and sixty yards, just short of the distance at which I had missed. An impala is the size of a small white-tail while a kudu bull weighs as much as an elk, yet Stuart had placed the bullet in the vital triangle behind the elbow, killing the animal instantly.

"Great," I said, trying to mean it.

Karim drove us over to Stuart and Steve and Harry.

"Here comes the photographer," Steve said as I climbed down from the hunting car. Stuart had been feeling bad for me about the kudu. As I did my best to congratulate him on his outstanding trophy, he was almost apologetic. Just a lucky shot, he protested.

HUNTERS ARE FOND of saying that hunting is not a competitive sport. Certainly, it should not be, mainly because it involves the death of animals. But if a particular hunter is a competitive person, as Hemingway was, he will probably regard the woods as a sports arena and shooting animals as the way to score. In *Green Hills of Africa* Hemingway represents himself as the competitive hunter, often petty, boastful, and resentful of the success of others.

To visualize him, imagine a handsome, strapping young man—mid thirties—with a dark mustache but no beard. He is already a famous writer; he is still more or less in love with his wife, Pauline, whom he refers to as P. O. M.—Poor Old Mama—and he worships his white hunter, the paternal "Pop." What he wants most on this safari, if not in life itself, is a kudu. The story opens with yet another unsuccessful hunt. Only a few days left before the end of the safari and the hunter's mood is deteriorating. In a long flashback Hemingway's friend Karl, who has also been obsessed with killing a kudu, returns empty-handed from eight days of hunting. His gloomy mood reflects Hemingway's, but Hemingway complains to Pop, "'Hell, he's got the best buff, the best waterbuck, and the best lion now . . . He's got nothing to worry about.'"

In the end, after many disappointments, Hemingway gets his kudu. Pop tells him that in his whole life he's seen only one bull killed with horns over fifty inches. This one measures fifty-two. Riding into camp, Hemingway cannot contain his joy. But there is Karl, just returned from his hunt.

> "What did you get?" I asked Karl.
>
> "Just another one of those. What do you call them? Tendalla."
>
> "Swell," I said. I knew I had one no one could beat and I hoped he had a good one too. "How big was he?"
>
> "Oh, fifty-seven," Karl said.
>
> "Let's see him," I said, cold in the pit of my stomach.
>
> "He's over there," Pop said, and we went over. They were the biggest, widest, darkest, longest-curling, heaviest, most unbelievable pair of kudu horns in the world. Suddenly, poisoned with envy, I did not want to see mine again; never, never.

To anyone who has hunted, Hemingway's jealousy of Karl and his kudu will be a familiar feeling. Most men, I suspect, whether hunters or not, can't help measuring horns. What matters is how you behave afterwards, no matter which end of the tape you come out on. As readers of *Green Hills,* we don't get to see how Hemingway behaved afterwards. He simply tells Pop the next morning that he's over it. Pop says, "We have very primitive emotions . . . It's impossible not to be competitive. Spoils everything, though." And the book ends. What we do get is the book itself, which is what Hemingway made out of the experience and the attitude that might otherwise have spoiled it—superb impressions of the Kenya bush and the behavior of animals, some of the finest in the language, and a condemnation of competitive hunting that he achieves, courageously, by an unfavorable representation of himself. And that is about all we can ask of any writer.

STEVE CARED LITTLE for the size of horns. What he wanted most was an opportunity to stalk game with his bow. That very afternoon, after ten days of looking for a puku with a respectable if not a trophy head, Karim and the trackers spotted one among the combretum. The animal was alone. Harry, Steve, and Stuart piled out of the vehicle, and Karim took the wheel. Harry directed him to swing out in a wide arc to the left in order to distract the puku. Ninety degrees around the perimeter of a circle, at the center of which the puku stood, Karim stopped. We were about four hundred yards from the animal and in full view of it. Its coat shone bronze red against the fading grass, which stood as tall as its white belly. If it was concerned about the vehicle, it showed no sign that it was but stared intently in the direction of the hunters, which it could not see. We could not see them either, but unlike the puku I knew that Harry was using the combretum bushes to cover their approach, as he had earlier with me and then with Stuart. Yet the puku seemed aware of some kind of danger. Because it couldn't see the men or smell them, it must have heard a scuff of boot against the dried soil. I couldn't understand why it didn't run, but I had seen deer behave in exactly the same way out of apparent curiosity.

Instead of running, the puku began a slow, dancing approach toward the combretum, stopping every step or two to stamp a foreleg and to wave its nose from side to side, seeking the scent that would confirm its sense of danger and send it bounding off.

"He thinks there's a lion," Karim said. "See how he's trying to get it to betray itself."

The puku was still too far away from the bush for Steve to try a shot, and it took a long time to get close enough. I found myself wanting to warn it, to shout "Watch out!"

Stuart, filming from Steve's point of view, caught it all on video. As the old buck's curiosity was leading it into danger, Harry and Steve were crouching behind the bush, Steve with an arrow in his bow, ready to draw. Later, as I watched the scene play out on the camera's little screen, I supplied from fresh memory the action Stuart had not been able to see from his vantage point. What I got was primal drama. The compound bow was too sophisticated to be considered a primitive weapon, and the broadhead was sharper than any stone, but the puku was the same animal that hunters stalked thousands of years ago, and at that moment the hunter himself was no different from his remote ancestors. The scene was a reenactment of the ancient rock paintings of southern Africa.

On the video Steve, while still kneeling, begins to draw the bow, then in continuous motion rises as he completes the pull and releases the arrow. When the puku ran, even Karim was fooled. "It smelled them," he said. But in a moment Harry and Steve emerged into the open. They examined the spot where the buck had been standing then proceeded in the direction in which it had gone. The video shows blood in the grass and then, beyond another bush, the puku dead.

Harry walked back out to where we could see him and waved to Karim to come on. As the hunting car lurched across the broken ground, I realized that by that stalk, as well as by the more dangerous stalk of the buffalo, Steve had staked a claim to the country. Which heightened my sense of the inadequacy of my experience of the Zambian landscape. I had not had the opportunity to appropriate it to myself sufficiently to feel that I belonged in it as a predator. The difference was not that Steve had killed, or even that he had killed with a bow; the difference was the intimacy with weather, terrain, and animals that hunting with a bow demanded and provided.

▼ ▼ ▼

Dark clouds lay low upon the Muchinga Escarpment. As the sun went down behind them, it rimmed the clouds gold, and gold beams radiated across the deepening sky. Harry stopped for us to admire the show with our cameras, and while we focused and snapped, the horizon turned dark red, as though to congratulate us on a successful day—two out of three, plenty of meat for the camp and impressive horns for Stuart and Steve.

We retrieved our jackets from a compartment behind the front seats. It was getting cold now, and as soon as Harry turned off this track onto the main road that led to the game scout village he would step on it.

Headlights of an oncoming vehicle appeared in the dusk, tourists headed for a lodge in the national park. A driver from the lodge had picked them up at the airport, as Harry had picked us up. They would stay in a camp like ours, on the banks of the Luangwa, and eat the same food—bushmeat, the natives called it—but they would not have killed it themselves. I wondered if it would taste the same.

Harry pulled over to the side to give the lodge vehicle room to pass, but instead of going on by, the driver slowed down and spoke, and Harry returned the greeting. The exchange lasted just long enough for me to get an impression of the men and women seated on the high benches in the rear. Armed with cameras and binoculars, they were decked out in catalog safari, and though we spoke, they ignored us, staring straight ahead, poker-faced—every one of them—as though that were the only way they could show their contempt for hunters.

"Bunny huggers," Harry laughed as we pulled away. "I don't know what they were talking about, but I bet we changed the topic of conversation."

When we reached the Milyoti Gate village Harry slowed up just enough to let Mbuluma jump off the back, and then we were speeding toward camp. I kept my eyes on the patch of white road illuminated by the headlights, watching for civets and other small animals. A mile beyond the village, something of color streaked across in front of us. Harry hit the brakes, turned on his spotlight, and swept the beam across the brush on the right. No more than twenty yards from the road crouched a leopard, a big tom, and his eyes in the light burned with green fire. Those eyes held us until he turned and slunk off into darkness.

"Bunny hugger" is the standard term professional hunters use to refer to tourists who come to Africa for photographic safaris. When Harry said it, it sounded almost affectionate, like a nickname, but

Steve made it sound like name calling. It became one of his favorite terms. Sitting around the fire after supper that night, I feigned offense. "I wish you'd stop using that word in my presence, Steve. Some of my dearest friends are bunny huggers. In fact, I'm proud to say that I'm one too."

Steve laughed. "You just think you are, Doc. What you really are is a predator. I can see it in your eyes. And I can't wait to get back to Athens and tell all those liberal bunny-hugger friends of yours that you've been operating under false pretenses. It didn't take you three seconds when I asked if you wanted to kill a kudu. I bet they'd love to hear that."

"But, Steve, I love to hug bunnies too. That may be too complicated for you, but that's what I'm trying to get you to understand. I could have been in that crowd we saw this afternoon. Very easily. Going to the Luangwa Valley to watch birds. And if you had met me in the road, you'd have dismissed me as a bed wetter. You don't have a clue about those people. One of them could have been a kudu hunter. In fact, the best hunters I know are bunny huggers too."

Harry was chuckling softly on the other side of the fire.

"Doc," Steve said, "you ever seen a squirrel in the middle of the road and a car coming?"

I decided to play professor. "Let me put a question to you," I said. "There's this guy in Sitka, Alaska, named Dick Nelson. He wrote a book about deer and deer hunting called *Heart and Blood*. He does most of his hunting on an uninhabited island offshore from Sitka, which means that he has to paddle a canoe across ten miles of open sea and often spend the night. He went over one day in June, which is not hunting season, paddling in a strong, cold wind and choppy water just because he'd had a sudden hankering to see and stalk deer. Without a rifle. On an island crawling with grizzlies. Actually, what he dreamed of seeing but wouldn't mention to anybody because the notion was so preposterous, was a doe giving birth to a fawn, which is something very few people have witnessed in the wild.

"Dick has this remarkable dog named Keta—a sort of small border collie type—that goes everywhere he does. Every dog I've ever owned would be an invitation to disaster in bear country, but Keta is perfectly obedient to voice commands and hand signals. They hadn't been there long when Keta picked up a scent—deer by the way she was acting. They stalked for a long time through spruce and muskeg, and the trail eventually brought them out onto a wide opening of marshy ground, and there in the midst of dry grass a couple of hundred feet away lay a doe. Dick didn't have a clue yet of what was about to happen, but he sat down to watch with Keta at his side. During the next hour, the doe got to her feet several times, lifted her tail, and arched her back. Eventually, it dawned on him that she was in labor. He could hardly believe it. When the fawn at last slid forth, he and the dog stayed put, and for the next hour, freezing his ass off, he watched every move the deer made. The wind was in his favor so she never sensed his presence. After a while Dick tied Keta to a bush and eased forward under the cover of trees and brush, stalking perfectly, until he reached the spot where the doe had given birth. Then he stepped out into full view, and the fawn came walking over to him on its wobbly little legs. He said it was no bigger than a cat. When it was close enough for him to touch, the doe, who still had not picked up his scent, put herself between him and her baby, and Dick just eased on back into the woods.

"Now here's the question: Is Dick Nelson a bunny hugger or a hunter? Or a squirrel that can't decide which way to go?"

Steve laughed. "You know this guy, Doc? I'd love to meet him some time."

"Until then," I said, "you might want to read his book."

WE SPENT the next morning driving the circle but we saw no game—no lion spoor at the baits, no antelope that Steve wanted to hunt, and no kudu, not even cows. We returned to camp for a late lunch and a quick nap. As I lay on my bunk in the cool chalet, I realized that if I was going to kill a kudu, an animal five times bigger than any I'd ever shot, and about that much more expensive, I needed if not a good reason at least a reason I could understand and explain. Hemingway was not enough. Neither was a mounted head. The head of my best white-tail buck had once hung above my desk at home, but after two years of watching it grow deader each day I gave it to the lodge used by our club. How much more a kudu. I could still change my mind.

THE AFTERNOON was as fruitless as the morning had been. Steve wanted to get back to camp early enough to shoot ducks and geese on the lagoon above the compound, but at the place where we had met the lodge tourists the day before we spied what we'd been looking for—three or four cows and a bull—perhaps a hundred yards off the road in open bush, feeding in the direction we were traveling. When Harry stopped, they looked up. They were so big that their heads seemed small, but their huge ears flared out, offsetting the discrepancy. The vehicle made them skittish and they began walking faster.

"Okay, Doc," Harry said. "There's your kudu."

Karim was already handing me the Weatherby.

"Whenever you feel ready."

Did he mean that I should shoot from the vehicle? Steve had not done that, and neither would I. To shoot from the vehicle would make a mockery of hunting, would reduce it to mere killing. Instead of a hunt to remember—an instant of African light, weather, dry bush smells, and such animals, incredibly present in that ambiance—I would be left with a taste of ashes in my mouth that I would never be able to spit out. Did Harry not understand that? If I was to shoot one of these splendid creatures, it would be by a fair stalk. I fumbled with the rifle long enough for the kudu to move into woodland.

Harry stepped down and beckoned to me. I followed him three hundred yards up the road, moving at a brisk pace, before he turned into the woods. The canopy was low and the ground covered by fallen leaves, as large as the leaves of sycamore and as dry as potato chips. It would be impossible to move quietly and almost as hard to see any distance at all. Harry was still hurrying. I kept up as best I could. Suddenly he stopped and set the shooting sticks. I was looking down a long open corridor through the woods, but I saw no kudu. Then came a cow, her hornless head seeming too small for her body, her neck too slender. Then came another and another. I had my eye to the scope, confident that the bull would be following his ladies, but the parade of cows passed and those great spiraling horns I'd expected never appeared. I was breathing hard, both from excitement and exertion.

"He's smart," Harry whispered. "Hand me the rifle."

I took the shooting sticks and followed as he tried once again to outflank the kudu. When at last he stopped, he pointed to the left. Amongst heavy green vegetation, a tail flicked. I nodded. Harry leaned across my shoulder and barely whispered, "Can you make that shot?"

I nodded and pointed to the ground, meaning that I wanted to sit. Harry nodded back and handed me the rifle as I squatted, but in the exchange the rifle slipped and struck the ground stock first with a clatter that seemed to shake the woods. The kudu must have heard that, I thought, but Harry whispered, "He's still there" and picked up the rifle. Now I could see enough of the gray shoulder to imagine the form of the entire animal. With my elbows resting on my knees I searched through the scope for a target. I had a small window of brush to aim through, but in the window was that gray shoulder. The hold was steady. I took a deep breath and squeezed slowly as I released it. In the roar of the shot the kudu bounded away. Harry put his hand on my back and said, "You missed."

"I don't see how I could have. I was steady on his shoulder. How far was it?"

"Eighty yards."

We followed the path of the kudu for a hundred yards or more to make sure there was no blood. Satisfied, Harry turned toward the road. I trudged along in silence as the late afternoon waned into dusk. When we reached the expectant faces at the vehicle, Harry said, "Missed." Nobody said a word.

VII

▼▼▼▼▼

WE APPROACHED the lion bait late in the morning. The track wound through open forest, twisting along the course of a sand river that separated the hunting concession from the national park to the north. The banks of the river were thickly wooded but from time to time the trees thinned out, permitting a view of the open plain on the other side—a different habitat. Now and then the track swung in close to the steep bank of the deep, dry channel. At one point a black raptor as large as an eagle rose from a sandbar in the shaded bed and labored his way up through the trees. It was a species I had not seen, but neither Harry nor Karim noticed it so the eagle went unidentified. From woods on our right small groups of zebra stood and watched as we bounced past, and once a large herd of impala crossed in front of us, each animal taking flight in turn as it reached the road, the herd strung out in a long, unbroken stream with a constant wave in it, as though the road were an obstacle in a steeplechase.

After a couple of miles the track turned away from the dry river bed and entered a meadow of long, yellow grass, open except for scattered tall trees. From one of the trees on the far side of the meadow Harry had hung a ripe quarter of hippo, hoisting it aloft by a cable attached to the rear bumper of the Land Cruiser. We found the bait astir with clustered vultures. At our approach they launched themselves grudgingly on dirty wings, losing altitude before swooping up to perch on limbs of nearby trees, while birds on the ground departed with ungainly hops, like people with their arms tied behind their backs. From a tree off to the left, which occupied only the corner of our eye, something stirred. A creature of rich color, its form no more defined than a spill of liquid, poured straight down the trunk and at the last instant sprang forth to the ground. Someone said, "Leopard!" and it was as though the naming of the cat stopped it in its tracks. For perhaps two seconds the leopard froze, its face turned toward us. Then it vanished, making a crease through the yellow grass.

And then we saw why it had been in the tree. From under the bait a black-maned lion got to its feet and walked away, its head lowered, and disappeared into the bush. The trackers in the rear of the vehicle came to life, more excited than they had been by any game we had seen thus far. They pointed in the direction the lion had gone and spoke to each other in whispers. "Nkalamo," they murmured, and I could feel their energy. Harry swung away from the bait in a wide circle and stopped on the side of the meadow where we had entered. He spoke to Demetrius and Silas in Nyanja then explained his plan to Steve. If they were to hunt the lion that afternoon, there was no time to construct a *machan*, or tree stand. They would have to build a ground blind now, as quickly as possible, and return at four.

To avoid disturbing the scene, we collected poles and grass from a site four or five miles away. Demetrius and Silas, working with the same traditional, handmade axes they had used to hack the buffalo in half, soon cut and trimmed a couple of dozen saplings and gathered great bundles of grass ten feet long. Karim made two trips hauling the materials, the grass overhanging the rear gate of the vehicle like a sweeping tail. Harry and Steve meanwhile had selected the site for the blind and paced off its dimensions. It was to measure six feet by six and stand within a thirty-yard bowshot of the bait.

Turning their axes into spades by removing the blade from the heavy mopani wood and inserting it butt-first into the end of the shaft, Demetrius and Silas chipped away at the hard gray dirt, making shallow holes for the uprights. When the frame was lashed together, it resembled the flimsy huts children build. As security against a charging lion, the blind was a joke, but concealment, not security, was its purpose. Still, the chances were about even that the lion, if wounded, would attack. Even if Steve placed the arrow in a vital spot, the lion could cover the distance between itself and the blind in two bounds. Any noise from the hunters, even the twang of the bow string, would betray their location.

The men lashed bundles of grass to the frame, leaving a narrow portal at the back and small windows for bow and camera in front. Then they camouflaged the blind with broken green branches and we returned to camp.

THE HUNT Harry planned was probably the riskiest of the safari, more dangerous even than the buffalo, but it was not reckless. As a professional hunter, his first responsibility was the safety of his client, and he had his livelihood to consider. Two years earlier a PH in Zambia had suggested to his client that they walk from a lion blind back to camp rather than wait to be picked up. It was dark, but the camp was so close they could see the lights of the dining hut. In that short distance, they blundered into a cow elephant and her calf, and the client, whose khaki outfit made him more conspicuous, was trampled to death. The PH surrendered his license.

As for the lion hunt, Steve's bow increased the uncertainty of an already unpredictable situation. Harry had confidence in his .458 Winchester, but he knew better than most the explosive speed of a wounded lion. The lion that mauled him the year before had come so fast across the open ground between them that Harry had had time for only one shot. A big male wounded by an arrow would be even harder to stop. And even if the lion didn't charge, Harry was pretty sure he would have to follow it into the bush, for that was his second professional responsibility. He was quiet at lunch and when he finished he went straight to his chalet.

I WAS STRETCHED OUT on my bunk enjoying a breeze that was sifting through the grass walls of the hut when Stuart came in. He sat down on the foot of his bed. "You awake, Doc?"

I opened my eyes.

"Do you think you know how to operate this camera?"

"I suppose I could learn. Why?"

"I want you to film the lion hunt this afternoon."

Stuart was a thoughtful young man, so soft-spoken and agreeable that you sometimes had to look around to be sure he was still there. The only thing we could find to tease him about was his conscientious concern with getting good footage. He was obsessed with the camera, and he was a perfectionist. Good footage was all he wanted.

Now he was asking me to take his place at the camera window of the lion blind. "I just want you to see the lion, Doc."

I couldn't tell whether he was feeling generous because of his outstanding shot on the impala or sorry for me because I'd missed the kudu. He was generous by nature and sympathetic too.

"Thank you, Stuart. I'd love to. You reckon it's all right with Harry?"

"I think Steve was going to mention it to him."

As it turned out, Harry was not comfortable with the idea. He doubted that I was spry enough to scamper up a tree should the need arise, and he didn't want to have to worry about an old man in addition to his other concerns.

"Harry's superstitious about this lion," Steve told me. "He thinks he knows him, thinks he's hunted him before, and it was that way with the one that mauled him. Harry is convinced that that lion knew him. He's worried that this one does too. He said you could take Stuart's place, but you're going to have to be dead silent."

There are ancient superstitions concerning the nature of lions among the people of south-central Africa. Stuart Marks, the anthropologist/biologist who once lived for a year with the Bisa tribe of the Luangwa Valley, says in his book *The Imperial Lion* that the Bisa traditionally recognize three kinds of lions—the natural, which people hunt and tourists photograph; the spiritual, which is the reincarnated spirit of a chief charged with protecting a place; and the imperial, or witchcraft, lion—*nkalamo ya kutuma*—which sorcerers use to attack specific people. I doubted that Harry believed in witchcraft, but this lion made him uneasy for reasons that were not entirely rational, suggesting a range of dark possibilities.

WE ARRIVED at the blind a few minutes before four o'clock, disturbing the vultures feeding on the bait. Again, they flapped off to the nearest perches, settling in to wait us out with hunched shoulders and sleepy patience. The trackers rolled out two single mattresses inside the blind, making a wall-to-wall bed. Steve with his bow, Harry with his rifle, and I with the camera entered and arranged our gear. Karim, Stuart, and the trackers made a noisy commotion of leaving, so that the lion, probably lying somewhere on the perimeter of the meadow and watching our every move, would think that everyone had gone.

Without speaking we lay back on the mattresses, shoulder to shoulder and tried not to even breathe. Karim was to return in two hours, just after dark.

The sun stood behind us, but its rays touched the interior and turned the air to dusty gold. There was nothing to see but sky, an overhead square framed by the walls of the blind—at first a flat patch of blue, but the longer I looked the deeper it became until I found myself at the funnel end of a vortex of azure shot through with shimmering light. The column of air was alive, made dimensional by insects that zoomed back and forth across the opening or buzzed at higher levels and by a speck or two that might have been floaters in my eyes except for the perfect circles they described far, far above.

SOON AFTER HER ARRIVAL in Kenya, Isak Dinesen became a trophy hunter. She could not live, she said, without collecting an outstanding specimen of every kind of animal. But during the last ten years of her stay she did no hunting at all unless the people on her farm needed meat. "It became for me an unreasonable thing, indeed in itself ugly or vulgar, for the sake of a few hours excitement to put out a life that belonged in the great landscape." That scruple applied to all animals except lions. "But lion hunting was irresistible to me. I shot my last lion a short time before I left Africa."

As I lay in the blind that afternoon with nothing to do but look up at the sky, I remembered my daughter's vexing question, "Antelopes, okay, but why leopards and lions?" Dinesen has an answer, though I doubt it would satisfy my daughter or many other people who have not been there. Of hunting generally she says that it is "ever a love affair. The hunter is in love with the game, real hunters are true animal lovers. But during the hours of the hunt itself, he is infatuated with the head of game which he follows and means to make his own. . . . Only, in general, the infatuation will be somewhat one-sided."

Except in the case of lions.

> But a lion-hunt each single time is an affair of perfect harmony, of deep, burning, mutual desire and reverence between two truthful and undaunted creatures, on the same wave-length. A lion on the plain bears a greater likeness to ancient monumental stone lions than to the lion which to-day you see in a zoo; the sight of him goes straight to the heart. Dante cannot have been more deeply amazed and moved at the first sight of Beatrice in a street of Florence. Gazing back into the past I do, I believe, remember each individual lion I have seen—his coming into the picture, his slow raising or rapid turning of the head, the strange, snakelike swaying of his tail. "Praise be to thee, Lord, for Brother Lion, the which is very calm, with mighty paws, and flows through the flowing grass, red-mouthed, silent, with the roar of the thunder ready in his chest." And he himself, catching sight of me, may have been struck, somewhere under his royal mane, by the ring of a similar Te Deum: "Praise be to thee, Lord, for my sister of Europe, who is young, and has come out to me on the plain at night."

The walls of grass warmed by the sun gave off a fragrance that sweetened the air we breathed, but when the breeze shifted, it brought the foul, clinging odor of rotten hippo.

Harry was certain that the lion would come back, for we had interrupted its feeding that morning. It had probably gone to water and then returned to the vicinity of the bait to lie in the shade until sundown. The slant of golden light was advancing up the grass walls, leaving us in shadow. I listened hard for any stirring, any rustling from the unseen world outside.

There were six—no, eight—specks in the sky. I blinked twice and there were twelve, and now they were larger than specks. A darker form sailed across the open space overhead, and I could see the set wings and the drop of the crooked neck and hear the wind in its stiffened primaries. They were multiplying faster than I could count, spiraling down along the edges of a warm updraft. The specks I had first noticed had been several miles high. Yet from that altitude they had seen the quarter of hippo hung against the trunk of a tree. They must have. They can't smell. I was witnessing a marvel.

Or had they seen us instead, the three of us, lying side by side as motionless as the dead?

The first rank of vultures was low enough now for identification, the dihedral of their wings rocking back and forth. Four or five species occur in eastern Zambia, but only the white-backed—from below, a plain, undistinguished bird—is abundant. White-backs were all I was seeing, but I was hoping for the uncommon species, the hooded, the white-headed, and the lappet-faced. I was not familiar enough with African vultures to identify them easily, but I remembered that the hooded was noticeably smaller than the others and that the lappet-faced from beneath showed conspicuous white legs.

A bird planed right over the blind, all but brushing the tops of the grass, and crash-landed with an ungainly thump within a few feet of us. Maybe the turbulence of its wake wafted to us the odor of rotten hippo, but when I smelled it I no longer gave a damn about ornithology. These were buzzards. Across the quick window above us they sailed, one after another, dropping their landing gear, setting their stubby tails. My eye ascended an unending spiral, as far up as I could see. And more specks were gathering. For the first time since arriving in Africa I remembered that I had cancer.

Darkness was moving up the grass wall, revealing the progress of sunset, and the dome above was tinged with a faint carmine wash. It was time for the lion. I had no fear of it at all, but the nasty vultures whose shadows swung across the blind deepened the gloom in which

I lay. They were out there by the score now, all over the meadow, hissing and squawking as they fought each other for scraps of carrion, making a dry rustle with their feathers.

In spite of the effects of four years of hormone therapy, I had been feeling unusually good during the last two weeks. The cancer had never made me sick, and I was feeling as strong now as I had at any time since the diagnosis. If I had had to escape a lion, I think I could have generated enough adrenaline to scamper up a tree. But being pinned motionless on my back in the blind watching vultures descend as though I were the main attraction reminded me that while the cancer had been suppressed it was not eradicated. Barring spontaneous remission or divine healing, which may be the same thing, it would someday get the better of me. Given the inevitability of death, I would take the lion.

With the setting of the sun, the descent of vultures ended, and darkness banished them to their foul roosts. The meadow was silent. The bowl of sky turned to indigo, and stars appeared, twinkling diamonds suspended in deep space. Nighttime hunters began to stir. I heard a distant yipping of hyenas, the bark of a zebra, a shrill bird call which may have been that of an owl. And then, from far away toward the eastern hills, came the faint roar of a lion. Steve clutched my arm. In a moment it came again. I was listening hard. And suddenly a huge sound shook the blind, shook the night itself—a deep yawning resonance that swelled into a louder, vibrant roar and ended in a descending series of throat-clearing coughs. And it came from right behind us.

I don't know why writers try to describe in language the roar of a lion. My attempt is no better than many I have read and not as good as some. It should be enough to say that when the lion is close you experience the roar more fully in your groin than your ear. That you find yourself in a circle with your primeval forebears, huddled shoulder to shoulder around a feeble fire. That you find yourself in the cave.

I had no idea how close this lion was, but he was not far away. He roared again, and he was closer. Harry rose slowly to his feet, a firm grip on his .458. The lion roared again and Harry pumped his fist. I couldn't see his face in the dark but I could almost feel the heat of his fever. He might have been apprehensive before but not now. His excitement was incandescent. The lion was walking—I could hear his steps—he was passing by the blind. His breathing was raspy.

Fear was not what I felt. It was more like the vulnerability bred into the bones of our kind through millennia of such nights as this. That part of me was feeling through the grass walls of the blind, sensing with my whole body the real presence of the lion.

On the Lion Panel of the Chauvet Cave appears one of the most astonishing paintings in all of Pleistocene art—three lions in profile, one superimposed upon another, stalking in precise alignment. The artist-shaman-hunter who wrought that image had heard the roaring of lions every night of his life, he had encountered the mystery of animals, and it galvanized his perception of the relationship between them as one of predator and prey. Whether or not the experience made the drawing better is not the point. The point is that it made it necessary.

I suspect that one who is fortunate enough to stand before the Lion Panel in the Chauvet Cave is close to the reality of lions, but all I know for certain is that I was. The experience was both visceral and psychological, or neurological in a way that connects body and soul. Beyond that I can't say. If the lion stood for something more than itself, as it does for the Bisa people, I don't know what it was—only that I feared no evil, and my impulse, from whatever part of me it came, was to praise the Lord of creation. Praise be to thee, Lord, for Brother Lion, who waketh me from slumber and restoreth my distracted heart.

There was a faint noise of a motor and then the rattle of the approaching Land Cruiser. Headlights swung across the blind and restored me quickly to the ordinary night.

VIII

THE MORNING AFTER our evening in the lion blind, I woke up wanting to kill a kudu. I'm not saying it was the lion that changed my attitude. Maybe the sequence was mere coincidence. But there it is. I entered the blind still uncertain and vaguely apprehensive about having to make a perfect shot before an audience, and I rose from my bed the next morning, after the roar of the lion, with a clear head and a clear heart, calm and ready to go.

It was colder than it had been. I pulled a heavy jacket from my duffel bag, walked over to the dining hut to pour a second cup of coffee, and took it steaming out to the fire pit patio. The river held dominion in the twilit landscape, shining like a sheet of metal, brighter than the wooded banks on the other side or even the white sandy beach that lay between me and the water, and doves began to call, the harsh three syllables of the turtle dove, the sweet, descending notes of the emerald-spotted. I hoped no one would join me. Participating in the dawn with calling doves and flights of geese and storks against the flush of the sky was my morning devotion.

Today I would kill a kudu. I would make a good shot and kill him clean, and everything would be as it should.

A raucous flock of wood hoopoes swept through the trees of the compound, their clamor overpowering the doves. At the same time a troop of baboons came filing along the beach in the half-light, their forms in silhouette against the glowing sand, swinging along on all fours, holding their kinked tails aloft, with infants clinging to the backs of their mothers. They had survived another night of leopard terror and were headed now for the lagoon above the compound where they would spend the day rooting for tubers in the bright green Nile lettuce.

It was time to get my boots on and to gather up my gear—camera, monopod, binocs, and the bag that held sunscreen, film, bird guide, and any meds that might be needed. When Harry started the Land Cruiser, he expected everyone to be on hand. By the time I climbed into the vehicle Silas and Demetrius had installed the cooler and hung the firearms on the gun rack. Now they were standing in the back smoking hand-rolled cigarettes, speaking quietly to each other of what the day might bring. I inhaled their secondhand smoke as it drifted by and with it an anticipation of large animals.

As Harry backed the vehicle around and headed toward the gate, he sailed a pack of cigarettes over the fence and into the kitchen compound. From my high seat I watched the dash and scramble of the staff.

WE STOPPED at the village to pick up Mbuluma. Blue mopani wood smoke from several cooking fires permeated the chill air. While we waited for him to come, small children gathered in the doorways of the compound fence and held out their hands, emboldened by days of successful begging. Steve, who kept a bag of sweets by his seat, flung two handfuls toward them, and they scrambled for them as the kitchen staff had scrambled for the smokes. Mbuluma came walking toward us along the side of a fence, in no hurry lest he compromise the dignity of his position. He wore olive military fatigues, and on his shoulder he carried the battered rifle with the welded-on front sight—the only rifle in camp, Harry had told us, and no more than five bullets to go with it. Mbuluma took his responsibility as game scout very seriously. I had never seen him cut up with Demetrius and Silas, who often teased each other but never him. "Bwanji," we said. He pointed to the sandy road by the front tire and said to Harry, "Nkalamu." A lion had walked through the middle of the village during the night. Harry leaned out from the driver's seat for a better look. "Female," he said.

We came upon the lions about two miles beyond the village—a female and three grown cubs, one of them showing a wispy promise of mane. They were lying in the early sun a hundred feet off the road, yellow brown in the tawny grass, watching us with unblinking eyes. I wondered if they posed a danger to the cyclists and pedestrians who traveled back and forth between their villages and Mfuwe. "Not in the daylight," Karim said. "But you wouldn't want to walk this road at night."

The black-maned lion of the day before was the only big male we had so far seen any sign of. Harry turned onto the track that led to the bait where we had built the blind. As we entered the meadow, a cloud of vultures rose from the bait and the ground around it, and the dry flapping of their dirty wings contaminated the air. Most of them settled on branches of nearby trees to await our departure. The flesh of the hippo quarter had been almost consumed. Little was left but a thick cowl of stiffened hide and a dark stain on the ground below it. "We need more bait," Harry said.

Harry had sent part of the safari outfit several days before to set up a fly camp in the hills, thirty miles to the east. "A good place for lions," he had assured us. He had been checking in with them by radio every day, but so far the fly camp had found no spoor either. And their bait too was being eaten by females, young lions, hyenas, and vultures. Steve had been allowed a second hippo, which he had taken several days ago, and Harry had used most of the buffalo for bait as well. And still no lion. We had a little more than a week to go, and he was getting anxious.

The return trip took the rest of the morning—another rough ride across the combretum plain, but now that I was eagerly scanning the aisles and openings for kudu we saw no animals at all. What we did see was a spiral of vultures, which indicated a lion kill. Harry turned from the track and headed across country, pursuing every possibility of locating a grown male. The vultures dispersed as we approached. To our surprise we found only a scrap of hide—no meat, not even a skull or bones. A narrow chalk-white stripe against the pale brown hair identified the species. "Kudu," Harry said. "Lions must have drug it away."

Even a female kudu is a big animal, weighing as much as or more than a lioness. Yet here, apparently last night, one or more of the cats had brought down the antelope, twisting its neck and shutting off its windpipe. I wondered if the lions we had seen earlier were the ones that had made the kill.

As we sat around the fire after supper that night, Steve asked Harry what the plans were for the next day.

"We need bait and the camp needs meat. One kudu will serve both purposes. So pray for a kudu. And pray for a lion."

That's what the safari has come down to, I thought. Lion and kudu. But to get a lion we have to get a kudu first, to use for bait, whether I shoot it or Harry gives up on me and asks Steve to take it. I don't think Steve would agree to that because he knows how bad I want it now, and it's Steve's call not Harry's.

You'd better be careful about wanting it too bad, another voice warned. The safari has already been a great experience. You don't want to ruin it by making everything depend on a kudu.

The next day we drove up to the fly camp in the hills so that Harry could deliver supplies and materials. I welcomed the change of scene, rolling country with large outcroppings of rock and boulders and hills that stood against the sky, but the landscape seemed empty of both animals and birds. For the first time in two weeks the sky was overcast. "Good country for kudu, Doc," Harry said. "Keep your eyes open."

I did, but the only animal we saw during the five-hour round trip was an antelope the size of a lap dog that bounded across the road in front of us. "Grysbok," Harry said. "Rare and nocturnal too. The first one I've seen here." I had caught no more than a glimpse of the creature, but that was enough to make me wonder that a cousin of the eland and the kudu could be so small.

On the way, Harry slowed down from time to time to allow Demetrius and Silas to set fire to the long grass. On the return trip several hours later we drove through a scorched and smoking landscape. In some places fire still crackled, and in the ashy heat waves that rose above the flames drongos and rollers hovered in their search for insects.

THE NEXT MORNING we entered upon the same old circuit through the combretum plain. We had not seen a kudu bull in three days. That didn't mean they weren't out there. We were just missing them on our rides through. I wished it were possible for Harry to drop me here at the edge of the plain, with only Karim or Demetrius for company, and pick me up on the other side just before dark. Then I could hunt as I had once hunted deer, alone and on foot, easing into the wind with the whole morning and miles of country before me. The law would not allow that, of course. A client had to be accompanied in the bush at all times by a professional hunter, for good and obvious reasons—elephants and lions to begin with. It would be easy enough to stumble upon a lion kill out there or to blunder into a herd of cows and calves, as we had the first time I missed.

What was bothering me was not the possibility of missing out on a kudu, but the image I had presented to the tourists the other day. I didn't care so much about what they thought as about what they thought they were seeing—a white American trophy hunter in camouflage, wealthy enough, they would have assumed, to pay a professional to drive him around the bush, to spot animals for him, and to tell him what and when to shoot. The difference between their perception and my sense of myself as a hunter was on the inside—a mind and heart that had sought to justify hunting by learning as much as possible about the countryside in which the hunt occurred. Through the years that I hunted deer in the floodplain of the lower Savannah River, I learned the terrain and the weather in all seasons; I knew the names of the birds that flew south in the fall and returned to nest in the spring; I knew their songs. I learned the names of trees and wildflowers and insects. For such knowledge is a way of loving, and only love, I had thought in those days, could justify the spilling of blood.

By pure coincidence the Savannah River land was property that had been owned in the nineteenth century by my grandfather's family. I discovered that they had been avid hunters, holding deer drives in the fall, shooting quail in the winter, and hunting turkeys in the spring. Though I hunted there as a paying guest of the current owners, I found deep satisfaction in continuing the practices of my forebears, conducting myself in the woods as I had been taught by my father, who had learned the code from his father, who had roomed in college with my other grandfather, the one who had grown up hunting deer in the same cane thickets I was hunting. The fact that my hunting was a participation in family tradition helped to authorize the activity and validate the killing.

Though I had not hunted in the past ten years, I had continued to believe that knowledge of the environment and consciousness of tradition were essential to hunting responsibly, at least for me, but here in the Luangwa Valley I could claim neither knowledge nor a cultural heritage. And without those qualifications, how was I any different from the camouflaged trophy hunter that the tourists thought they saw in the Land Cruiser? I could have told them that I was acquainted with Ernest Hemingway and Isak Dinesen and Peter Matthiessen, the tradition of white people who shaped their experiences of Africa into narrative, and that I was hoping to do the same thing if I could hunt and kill a kudu.

Green Hills of Africa begins and ends with kudu. In between, you get other kinds of hunting—lion, rhino, buffalo, and sable—and the competition motif runs all the way through, but it is the quest for kudu that gives the book its theme and structure. At the halfway point, Hemingway says of his hunting companion Karl, "his feelings about the kudu complicated the hunting." Because Hemingway shares those feelings, they complicate the narrative as well, and the result is a good book. But it takes an animal as majestic as a kudu to provide those complications. Toward the end, when there is only one day left, Pop hears from natives that kudu have been seen in an area he has never hunted. He has to leave for another camp, but he sends Hemingway off to the new area, saying, "I think this is a turning point. You'll get a kudu."

Hemingway responds, "It's just like when we were kids and we heard about a river no one had ever fished out on the huckleberry plains."

Pop asks how the river turned out, and Hemingway says they got there just before dark and he rigged his line with three flies and on the first cast hooked three trout. Pop calls him a "damned liar."

"I swear to God."

"I believe you. Tell me the rest when you come back. Were they big trout?"

"The biggest bloody kind."

"God save us," said Pop. "You're going to get a kudu."

And sure enough, Hemingway gets not one but two, each of them fifty inches or better.

I was in high school when I read *Green Hills of Africa* the first time. I doubt that I had ever heard of kudu before. If I had, it was merely as a name which evoked no image. But reading the book not only introduced me to the animal, it gave me a sense of the kudu as something extraordinary, splendid and elusive. Of all the animals Hemingway hunted in Africa, it was the one he wanted most, and when at last he came upon it, in the failing light of the last day, there was a magic in the encounter, as though an agency far beyond his skill or any man's dumb luck had brought the two together.

ON THE FIFTH DAY we entered the combretum plain from the other side, checking the second lion bait by the hippo pool where Steve had killed the buffalo. The morning was heating up early and there was little game. When Harry stopped, I figured we were taking a bathroom break, but he looked back at me and said, "Want to shoot that puku, Doc?"

About one hundred yards out to the left, browsing among the combretum, were a buck and two does that I had not noticed. But I didn't understand what Harry had in mind. Had he decided that my chances now of getting a shot at a good kudu were so remote that I should settle for a puku? Karim handed me the rifle and I started over the side, but Harry said, "Just go ahead and pop him from there."

I didn't like this, but either I was to do what Harry proposed or ask why, and this seemed not the time for questions and explanations. In any case, this was no kind of hunt. I wasn't sure what it was. I rested the rifle upon the padded roll bar and found the buck in the scope, reddish brown against the gray green of the combretum. His horns were no better than average. He turned broadside to me and the crosshairs steadied on a spot just behind the shoulder. I squeezed the trigger and the puku dropped. Karim clapped me on the back, but I felt no sense of the elation that comes when you make a good shot on an animal you want and have hunted well. Anyone could have made that shot, and what I had done was no different from shooting a goat in the yard.

Everybody piled out and started toward the puku. As we approached, the animal lifted itself onto its forelegs and struggled to escape. Had I been approaching a wounded deer, I would have stopped right there and delivered a killing shot, but this was not my show, if it had ever been, and I no longer had the rifle. Harry was yelling at the trackers in Nyanja, and though I didn't know the words I understood the impatience in his voice. Demetrius, Silas, and Karim sprinted forward and overtook the puku. Demetrius and Silas each grabbed a horn and pulled back the head, exposing the throat to Karim's knife. I turned away, but the animal bleated terribly—a deep, desperate sound that comes only when an animal knows it's about to die. Karim was "koshering" the buck, making it lawful for Muslims to eat, as he would have cut the throat of a lamb or a kid, but knowing that didn't help. Animals are not human, they are "other," and I was not one to anthropomorphize wild creatures, but the puku's bleat of terror had sounded human, too much as I would sound if my throat were being sawed open.

When the puku was dead, Steve said, "Let's see where you hit him." We walked over to where it lay, bleeding freely from its throat in the dusty grass. It was an old buck, its face scarred from fighting, and its thickly ridged horns were worn and stubby. I saw no wound.

"Oh, here," Steve said. I had hit the puku in the spine, near the base of its tail, and paralyzed its hindquarters. At no more than a hundred yards.

That's it, I decided. No more shooting for me. Without saying anything, I turned and started back to the vehicle. Harry came up alongside me. "He's old, but he'll taste good."

"We harvested him for the table?"

"Mbuluma said the village needs meat. He asked if we could shoot a puku for them. We'll take the loin and give the rest to them."

That eased my suffering a little, but it did nothing for the embarrassment of another bad shot.

Back at the car Mbuluma shook my hand, grabbed my thumb, and smiled. "Zikomo kwambiri, bwana." Thank you very much.

As I was about to climb the ladder up the side of the vehicle, Steve drew me aside. "I saw what you've been doing wrong," he said. "You're anticipating the shot and pulling off. Next time, keep your eye to the scope and follow through."

WITH THE CARCASS of the puku in the back of the vehicle, we opened the cooler and passed out sandwiches and cold drinks. The kitchen staff might have packed two or even three kinds of sandwich that day, probably guinea fowl and any impala left over from last night's supper, but by an unspoken custom, you ate whatever you grabbed or were handed from the cooler. I could tell even before I unwrapped the tinfoil that I had drawn sardine. No point in asking if anyone wanted to swap. Karim was popping bottle caps on the bumper. As I waited to hand him mine, Demetrius tapped me on the shoulder. "Open?" he asked. I passed him the Coke and with no effort at all he put the cap in his mouth, twisted it off with his teeth, and spit it on the ground.

Harry wolfed down his sandwich, stuck his orange soda between his thighs, and started the engine. Before I had finished my sandwich, which I was eating as slowly as possible, he stopped again. Karim removed the .300 Weatherby from its case and handed it to Steve who was already on the ground. Harry stood on the seat and scanned the combretum through binoculars, and Stuart gathered up his camera gear. Everyone but me seemed to know what was going on.

"This might be a roan, Doc," Harry explained. "Or maybe a kudu. I couldn't tell."

The roan is a large antelope, almost as big as a kudu, with a strikingly patterned face. Though Steve had a permit for one, they were scarce in our area, and so far we had not seen any. But roan or kudu, Harry was telling me that he and Steve had decided that Steve would take the shot.

Harry asked Demetrius a question in Nyanja.

"Inde," Demetrius said. "Pulupulu."

"Come on, Doc," Karim said. "It's a kudu."

Steve handed me the rifle. "Remember now. Follow through."

With the smell of sardine still in my beard I fell in behind Harry for another stalk in the burning sun, out across the dry grass and rough black cotton soil of the combretum plain. Steve followed me and Stuart was back there somewhere, maybe Karim too. A regular damned gallery to watch this performance. This is it, I thought, one way or the other. If I miss this time, I'm through.

I kept my eyes on Harry's heels and concentrated on keeping pace. I didn't have much sense of the distance we were covering, but we walked for what seemed like ten minutes or more, and I was beginning to breathe heavily. Then Harry's gait changed, he crouched, and his body assumed the intensity of a stalking cat. The tension that held him poised communicated itself to me, and I coiled too. With one quick movement he stepped from the cover of a combretum and placed the cane tripod. Before I knew what was happening, I was looking through the scope at a group of cows more than one hundred yards away.

Where is the bull?

I counted three, maybe four animals. They were bunched on the far side of a large bush, some facing one way, some facing the other, and their bodies, partly concealed by the bush, seemed to merge into one tan biomass with several pairs of huge ears perked and listening.

They see us now. Where is the bull?

A kudu stepped out from behind the bush and walked in front of the cows, from left to right. He was a darker animal and he had horns, but they were noticeably shorter than those I had been seeing.

"He's not very good, is he?" I whispered.

"Wait," Harry said.

I lifted my eye from the scope. A flock of lovebirds swept across the open space between us and the kudu, flashing green in the sun, and I heard turtle doves in the distance. The young bull had turned to face us now, and his ears too stood out from his head.

Then I put my eye to the scope again and there he was, as though the scope itself had created him—a great bull kudu, dark and majestic. He filled the field of view. And his horns. What a weighty crown. Yet he lifted his head effortlessly, and the horns swayed with the movement, as the masts of a ship sway with the rolling of the sea.

The bull stood, presenting to me his profile—the shot hunters dream of—but Harry whispered, "Wait. There's a cow behind him." She was directly behind him, facing the direction from which he had come, her head held high above his rump, and she too was watching. If I hit him behind the shoulder, the bullet might well pass through him and wound or kill her. "Wait," Harry said.

The young male separated himself from the group and moved off to the right, then turned and faced us head on. The old man's son, I thought, edgy and alert, trying to act like a grownup, or maybe his *askari*, as they say in Swahili, a young friend who keeps watch for danger. I was afraid that he might sound the alarm any second. And that would be that. Startled, they would flush like a covey of quail.

The air shimmered with light, and the sun beat down upon my uncovered head. Sweat stung my eyes. All I could smell was damned sardine juice. In my beard.

The bull did not so much as quiver but stood frozen, blurred by an aura of light into an icon of Africa.

"Wait," Harry whispered.

It would have been so easy. I had been holding steady, remembering everything—take a deep breath, slowly release it, slowly squeeze the trigger, and keep your eye to the scope, follow through. I was in accord with everything within me that it would take for me to shoot.

The bull lowered his head as if to graze. I wiped sweat from my eyes. Suddenly, he threw his head up and looked straight at us, as though he had heard something that made him nervous. An animal will stare at an unmoving, unfamiliar object for only a limited amount of time before it bolts. The kudu lowered his head again, as if in displacement anxiety, and began to graze again, but the cows and the young bull kept their vigil. All those eyes.

I was on him, steady on his shoulder. Without budging, I whispered, "I can take him any time."

"Wait."

He lifted his head once more. With the wind in our favor and unable to detect movement, he had still not perceived us as an immediate threat, but he was not comfortable. He turned his body one quarter toward us and sniffed at the breeze. The crosshairs were fixed on his shoulder. One more second and he would bolt. "Now," Harry said.

The report of the rifle was like a stick of dynamite going off in their midst, scattering them in all directions. By the time I recovered from the noise and the recoil, the bull had disappeared. Harry hurried forward, I in his tracks. I was sure I had hit him. The question was where. If this were another poor shot, we might be tracking for the rest of the day. The possibility made me feel sick. Suddenly, the bull came surging out from behind the combretum, forty yards away, right across our front, his great gray body struggling to take flight.

"Get up there, Doc. Get up there," Steve was yelling from somewhere behind me. I was running, the rifle at half port. The bull's hooves struck the ground, and his front legs buckled. He lunged forward and crumpled.

"He's down," I said to Harry, gasping for breath.

"Down doesn't mean dead," Harry said. "Come on." But after three steps he stopped, looked, then turned to me. "Nah, he's dead." He extended his hand and when I took it he pulled me into an embrace, a big grin on his face. Steve was laughing, pounding me on the back, and Karim came over and put his arm around my shoulder.

The kudu lay large and striped and bluish gray in the dry grass, and his lyre-shaped horns were splendidly symmetrical. His striped mane, the bristles stiff like the mane of a mule, extended from the withers to the base of the tail, and a pure white chevron distinguished his chocolate-colored face. Dark blood pulsed from his mouth, pumped by the last faltering beats of his heart, and pooled around his muzzle, staining the white beard. With the folded shooting sticks Harry gently touched the orb of his eye, as big as the eye of a horse, and Steve, beside himself with the gladness of great relief, was laughing, "You hammered him, Doc. A perfect shot, right in the heart." Stuart, with the camera to his eye, moved in close.

"They won't have to cut *his* throat, not the way he's bleeding," Steve said.

"No," I said, "Nobody's touching him."

They all laughed at that and clapped me again on my back. I appreciated their rowdy congratulations, but at that moment I would rather have been alone, just for a few minutes, to contemplate undistracted the magnitude of what I had done. Harry set up the tripod and I hung the rifle from it, as I had seen Steve do. Then I knelt by the kudu and traced with my index finger the narrow chalk stripes; I bent over to inhale the rich, musky animal smell of him, and my nose touched his coat, which was thin and lightly haired and warm from the sun.

The horns were coated with wet mud. I closed my hand around the ridged base of the left one, and its circumference more than filled my grasp, too big for my fingers to encircle. "Why does he have mud on his horns?" I asked Harry, squishing it off with my thumb and index finger.

"He's been swishing them in a mud puddle."

"I know but why?"

"It's just something they do sometimes."

I walked over to the place where the kudu had stood, and there behind the combretum bush was a shallow pond, its soft edges cut deep by many sharp-edged prints. The water was still swirled with mud where the bull had roiled it. I tried to picture the scene. Had he gone down on his knees to immerse his horns? I walked back to where he lay, twenty yards away. His knees were dry, but his hooves were caked, the mud already turning gray. Steve handed me a beer and I seated myself in a patch of shade to drink it, still wondering why the great bull had lowered his head to the water and buried his horns in mud.

"He's a good one, isn't he?" Steve asked Harry.

"Very good. He's an old bull, eight or nine, I'd say."

"How much will he weigh?"

"Seven hundred maybe."

I didn't care. I didn't even want to know the measurements of his horns, though I knew I would later. At that moment bare statistics had little to do with the magnificent reality lying in the grass. Lying right there, not twenty yards from where he was standing when I hit him. Before I finished the beer, Karim returned with the Land Cruiser. It came jouncing toward us across the broken ground with Demetrius, Silas, and Mbuluma standing in the rear. When they saw me, they all raised their arms above their heads and pumped their fists. I met them as they climbed down, and each man, even the dignified game scout, shook my hand, grabbing my thumb and smiling.

The trackers brought a jerry can of water to clean the mud from the horns, and Mbuluma began chopping away bunches of grass for unobstructed photographs. I opened another beer and listened to the doves, feeling complete and happy. *Tragalaphus strepsiceros, tendalla, mpulupulu, pulupulu, iqudu, koedoe, kudu.* I wanted to know the name of this animal in every language in which he had a name.

Part Four

THE TIMELESS CAMPFIRE

In proof of what the sun could do, I compared my own bronzed face and hands, then about the same in complexion as the lighter-colored Makololo, with the white skin of my chest. They readily believed that, as they go nearly naked and fully exposed to that influence, we might be of common origin after all.

DAVID LIVINGSTONE, *Missionary Travels*

We ourselves, in boots, and in our constant great hurry, often jar with the landscape. The Natives are in accordance with it, and when the tall, slim, dark, and dark-eyed people travel . . . or work the soil, or herd their cattle, or hold their big dances, or tell you a tale, it is Africa wandering, dancing and entertaining you.

ISAK DINESEN, *Out of Africa*

The drama of events is narrated as a fragment of history. Its repetition in time gives it a dreamlike quality. . . .
In Africa the whole clan gathers to hear Bushmen tell, sing, and re-enact episodes from the last hunt. The events are considered at once lightly and solemnly. Places are important—
they are the anatomy of space.

PAUL SHEPARD, *The Tender Carnivore and the Sacred Game*

IX

▼▼▼▼▼

On one of our infrequent trips into Mfuwe, Harry took us to a place of business called Tribal Textiles. It was not a shop but a small factory and craft outlet where members of a coop produced painted fabrics that ranged in size from napkins to bedspreads. A young British woman named Gillie had organized the coop several years ago in the belief that if local people could make a living with these textiles they would not have to snare animals to sell as bushmeat. The coop now employed about sixty people. Gillie took us on a station-to-station tour of the process. A man named Moses, one of a team of artists, was drawing a design on a square of white cloth that would be passed on to a painter who chose colors according to his whims. The painted cloths then went through several stages of drying, one of which was an all-day exposure to the sun. The finished products were stacked on shelves and packed in barrels. There were hundreds of them. Some of the larger ones Gillie hung on a clothesline for our inspection; others she spread on the cement floor. Each design was a vibrant kaleidoscopic dance of animals—elephants, giraffes, warthogs, zebras, kudu, elands, impalas, lions, guinea fowl, fish, and crocodiles—a rich bestiary of the Luangwa Valley rendered in the dry colors of the bush, baked in the African sun. And here and there among the animals, running in pursuit, were hunters, stylized black figures armed with bows and arrows—the very figures that were drawn in ancient times on the granite walls of southern Africa.

THE OLDEST ROCK ART in sub-Saharan Africa occurs along a belt of granite between the Zambezi and Limpopo Rivers, the northern and southern borders of present-day Zimbabwe. Most ethnographers agree that the images were made by ancestors of the San Bushmen, hunter-gatherers who were driven out of the area more than a thousand years ago by invading Bantu tribes. Unlike the Pleistocene art of southern Europe, which decorates the walls of deep caves, the southern African drawings usually appear on faces of sheltered granite, in shallow recesses, and beneath overhanging stone. Moreover, they include representations of humans, which are almost entirely absent in the European caves. In these drawings, in fact, people outnumber animals, but the people are almost always depicted in association with animals, which suggests that animals played a major role in the social and perhaps the spiritual lives of the societies that decorated the rock. The predominant relationship is that of the hunt.

At a site called Matobo in southwestern Zimbabwe there is a beautifully delineated, naturalistically rendered image of a kudu surrounded by more stylized figures of hunters. One of the hunters is crouched over as though he is stalking the animal. Another is kneeling and drawing his bow, and, though he is aiming away from rather than toward the kudu, it is his occurrence in proximity to the animal that matters, for these pictures are not realistic portrayals of actual events but depictions of archetypes.

The kudu bull looks exactly like the one I shot, but when I study the hunters I see not myself but native Africans, first Bushmen and then Bantu, whose lives for millennia depended upon such animals. I wonder how they thought and what they believed about the animals they killed. Did they regard them as meat on the hoof or as kindred spirits who offered up their lives for the life of the hunter? Did they believe that future success depended upon the purity of their attitude and their conduct in the hunt, or did they gloat over the death of the animal? The answers to such questions are lost forever. What we do know is that they recreated on the granite surfaces of their country the act of hunting—the hunter and the hunted in a timeless dance that occupied the center of their lives on this earth.

X

FROM OUR FIRST DAY in camp, Harry had made it clear that we were not to leave valuables in the hunting car or even hanging from posts in the dining hut overnight. The trackers put away the rifles and bows each evening when we came in, but we were responsible for keeping up with personal gear such as cameras, binoculars, and day-packs. Harry had never had a break-in at this or any other camp, and he didn't want his record broken now. He had put out word among the safari staff that the compound was off limits to the local people who fished up and down the river or moved along the narrow track that ran past the camp. Often these people stopped at the skinning hut below the compound to pass the time with friends who worked for the safari, and Harry wanted them to understand that any unau-thorized person caught within the compound, especially after dark, was subject to being shot on sight. I didn't know whether Harry ac-tually meant that or not; all that mattered was that the local people believe he did. Even so, we had a break-in and a theft the night after I killed the kudu.

I AWOKE that morning to a sweet dawn, my body strengthened by the meat of the animal I had slain. We had been eating game twice a day since Steve shot the impala, but, whatever the species of meat, the cook always prepared and served it either ground or chunked or stewed. Harry complained about the sameness of the recipes, but the cook told him that the animals we brought in were too small to yield the steaks he requested. But last night we were treated to kudu filet mignon.

Bernard brought me coffee as he did every morning. I pulled the mosquito netting from where it was tucked beneath the mattress and sat up in bed. It felt like the first morning after the last day of school and you had made all A's. I was going bird-watching. Karim was going to take me to the lagoon.

After an early breakfast Harry, Steve, and Stuart left on foot to stalk the river forest below camp. Steve was anxious for a bushbuck and there was a chance that they might spot a waterbuck as well. Karim and Demetrius and I climbed into the hunting car and headed upriver. When we arrived at the lagoon, Karim took a rifle from its case and handed it to Demetrius. It was the first time, I told Karim, that I had ever been bird-watching with an armed escort. He said he suspected it was the first time Demetrius had ever accompanied a birdwatcher into the bush.

The lagoon was a narrow oxbow that had once been part of the main channel of the meandering Luangwa. Cut off from the river now, it lay against the old bank, still and shallow, a shaded haven for birds and beasts. We scrambled down the embankment to the edge of the water, flushing ducks, geese, and herons, and found convenient roots to settle on. Karim and I identified open-billed storks, the beautiful little jacana—a bright spot of russet walking with widespread toes across the lily pads—and various herons, ibises, and waterfowl. Karim sat at my side, perched on the roots of a tree, as intent as I on enjoying birds, while Demetrius, the armed guard, stationed himself ten yards up the bank and waited out the whim of the American bird-watcher. Occasionally, Karim asked Demetrius what a particular bird was called in Nyanja. Soon Demetrius was pointing out birds to us.

A pied kingfisher, patterned in black and white, sallied out from its post across the way and hovered above the water, fluttering like a butterfly, twittering like a songbird. Instead of returning to its perch, it settled on a snag in the middle of the lagoon, directly in front of us, and fixed its dangerous gaze on the depths below. I had seen a pied kingfisher once on the Jordan River in Israel but only for a darting second. Here the diminutive bird offered itself up to my delighted eye.

The report of a rifle from below camp interrupted our outing. "Steve has meat," Karim said. "We'd better go." As we climbed the bank, Demetrius said something to Karim, who translated for me: "Demetrius says to tell you that he has never paid attention to birds before this morning, but you have made him interested. From now on, he says, he will notice birds wherever he goes."

We met the hunters walking up the narrow, grassy track toward the skinning hut, Steve, Stuart, and Harry leading the way, Mbuluma walking behind them with a bushbuck draped across his shoulders. Though Steve had had to use a rifle instead of his bow, he was nonetheless elated. He regarded the beautiful little forest antelope as a great prize.

When we drove into the compound, we were met by Bernard and the cook, who called Harry aside to report that thieves had come in the night and taken two of the mattresses used in blinds, a generator, a battery, and the satellite phone Steve had brought. The phone, which Steve had rented at an exorbitant rate, was a major loss.

Harry was not a demonstrative man, but no one could have missed the change in his demeanor. Anger smoldered in his eyes, and the line of his mouth grew tight. As soon as the bushbuck was cleaned, he said, we were going to Mfuwe. We would report the theft to the police and call on the Kunda chief Nsefu, which was the reason for taking the bushbuck. While Harry made a list and checked the camp for other missing items, we sat at the table drinking coffee and speculated on the break-in. The thieves must have come on foot or bicycle because there were no automobiles in the area. It would have taken several men to carry away so much, including the heavy generator, and where would they have stashed it? The camp was miles away from any village. What did they plan to do with the stolen items anyway, especially the telephone, which could not be used without knowledge of the code? Karim said Harry suspected an inside job, or at least cooperation by someone employed by the safari. He trusted none of them completely, not even Demetrius. If he should determine that anyone working for him had been involved, that person would not only be prosecuted, he would never work for a safari company again.

BECAUSE the Upper Lupande Game Management Area, where we were hunting, was closed to settlement and agriculture, its boundaries had become in my mind an invisible wall within which we could play safari without having to remember that this was the year 2000 and that another Africa lay all around us, dying of poverty, disease, and politics. The distribution of shoes had brought us into brief and superficial contact with that society, but since then we had remained isolated. Until this morning. What had happened, it seemed to me, was not merely a random act of a few desperate thieves, but an invasion of our little camp by an Africa that had a different definition of "real." I don't mean to suggest that the theft was an act of political protest against white Americans. It may have been, but I didn't think so. Whatever it was, it broke the bubble in which we had lived and hunted, and I began to feel surrounded by a larger context.

The police station at Mfuwe was housed in a small, one-story cinderblock building that sat inconspicuously in a row of similar structures. A hand-lettered sign was the only indication that this was the local constabulary. Harry pulled up in the driveway beside the building, and he and Karim went in. There was no shade where he had parked and the sun was hot. We hoped he wouldn't be gone long.

While we waited, people came and went, emerging from houses to water their gardens or moving along the dusty road. They paid no attention to us. A passing glance told them all they needed to know. Although they understood and even spoke English, which is the official language of Zambia, I had the feeling that if I asked them a question, they would answer in Nyanja.

Harry had little to say when he and Karim returned. The police were understaffed. They had no vehicle to take them so far out into the bush. But if Harry should catch the thieves and bring them in, they would be happy to make an arrest.

We headed down the macadam road built by former President Kaunda to connect the airport with his private lodge in the national park. After several miles, Harry turned off to the left in search of the compound where, he had been told, he would find the chief, but even if he found her he could not be sure that she was the right Nsefu. The former paramount chief, a man who had held that position for many years, had died two days before we arrived, and the succession had not yet been settled. The two principal claimants were young women, both matrikin of the dead chief and probably first cousins to each other. One had taken up residence in the chief's palace—a one-story brick ranch style house—and refused to yield to the other, who, the first one claimed, had killed the chief by sorcery. In fact, Harry believed, the chief had died of AIDS. Both women had appropriated the hereditary name Nsefu, which means "eland," and Harry didn't know which way to turn. A week before the old chief died, Harry had sent word to him that American clients were coming with shoes for his people. A week after our arrival the Nsefu who had moved into the chief's residence appeared at our camp with a few retainers and requested the promised shoes. Harry and Steve gave her a bag that had been held back in case of such a development, and she had left well-pleased. Two days later Harry heard from her rival that he had given the shoes to the imposter. Playing both ends against the middle, he had decided, since he couldn't recover the shoes, to appease the other Nsefu with a gift of the bushbuck. At the same time, he would ask for her assistance in catching the thieves.

At the end of the road we pulled into a spacious fenced compound and stopped in the sun. A modern one-story brick house dominated the enclosure, but five or six round grass huts of varying sizes stood scattered about the bare yard. Two women sat on mats in front of the brick house doing something with their hands, whether working with food or fabric I couldn't tell. Several small yellow dogs—the generic fyce of poor settlement edges throughout the world—lay in the shade while ducks and chickens pecked about the yard for stray morsels. Off to the right, beneath a grove of trees, sat three men and two women. The younger woman was heavy and wore a bright cloth around her head. Harry, Karim, and Silas climbed out of the vehicle and started toward the circle beneath the trees. When they had approached, all three knelt down, bowed, and clapped. One of the women must have been the chief Nsefu.

After a while two young men came over to the vehicle, took the skinned bushbuck from the back, and with each holding it by two legs they lugged the carcass across the yard to one of the grass huts. Right after that, the group beneath the trees, led by our men, came over to where we were parked. We climbed down, removed our caps, and greeted the chief—the heavy-set young woman—with bows and claps, which she received with royal dignity. Harry offered them all Coca-Colas from the cooler. The chief and two of her companions needed a ride down the road, Harry said. He invited her to take the seat at his side. The other two—a man and a woman—climbed up onto the bench while the rest of us crowded into the back.

The compound we visited was not the young woman's home but that of a sub-chief who was supporting her right to the throne. She and her friends were leaving to call on relatives several miles away, probably to enlist their support in the unresolved contest. As we rode, I studied the faces of the people we met along the way to see how they reacted to their new ruler being chauffeured in a safari car by a professional hunter who might as well have been a white man as far as they were concerned. A few stopped and clapped, many waved, but just as many paid no attention.

We pulled in at a busy roadside flea market, but the arrival of the chief caused no stir among the vendors and their customers. As she was thanking Harry for the lift, Steve presented a bag of pocket crosses and asked if she would like to have them. Her pretty brown face lit up as she reached for it.

Back in camp Harry reported that the chief-in-dispute had promised to issue an order stopping Kunda tribesmen from fishing in the Luangwa River both above and below the compound. But issuing such an order was one thing; enforcing it, especially in her tenuous circumstances, was another. Besides that, not all fishermen in the Lupande area were Kunda. Where members of other tribes were concerned, Nsefu had no authority. Harry announced a reward for information leading to the apprehension of the thieves, but he was not optimistic about recovering the stolen goods.

STEVE AND STUART AND I had been curious from the day we arrived in the valley about the Kunda people, how they regarded game animals, whether or not they hunted, or wanted to, and if so, where, what, and how. The Lupande area was their ancestral land. Until the coming of the British at the turn of the century, they had been free to live and plant and hunt here, but the colonial government claimed the animals for white hunters and set aside large tracts of land as game preserves. Independence had not improved the circumstances of local people in regard to hunting. The parks and game management areas—thousands of square miles—were still off limits. Harry had told us that the game department granted native Zambians a brief period to hunt, after the safari season ended and before the long rains inundated the valley, but even then they had to purchase a license which cost thirty-five dollars, an amount few local tribesmen could afford. When I asked Harry about their hunting, he said only that they poached, stalking buffalo with homemade muzzle loaders and setting wire snares for whatever happened to come along. Commercial poaching in the 1980s, which had completely exterminated the black rhinoceros in the Luangwa Valley and drastically reduced the elephant population, had been stopped, but subsistence poaching, which conservationists were now calling the bushmeat crisis, was threatening species throughout sub-Saharan Africa. If something wasn't done to stop it, Harry said, the safari business would soon be out of business.

Our visit to Mfuwe and the would-be Nsefu who had promised to stop Kunda people from fishing in the Lupande Management Area stirred up my interest in the local people and their attitudes toward safari activity. From then on, every impassive black face I met on the dusty roads that ran through the concession asked me what we were doing there. If I was to write about the experience of hunting in Africa, I was going to have to understand it not as the imitation

Hemingway adventure it appeared to be but in the context of ancient hunting traditions that the land had not forgotten. One day soon after our trip to Mfuwe, Demetrius said to me in English, "Bwana, you come back to Zambia, we take you hunting." That was an easy offer for him to make since such a thing could never happen for any of a host of reasons. But Demetrius had nothing to gain by making it except my goodwill, which he already had, and I had nothing to lose in taking it for approval. In any case, the notion flourished in my imagination. A writer named Eric Zency, whose essay "On Hunting" is as good on that subject as anything I've read, says, "Other tribes have a vocabulary, in language and ritual and belief, that lets each tale affirm the depths of meaning of the hunt." I might never be able to hunt with Africans as a hunter among hunters, but I wanted to learn their vocabulary and hear their tales, for it is only by such knowledge that one enters any particular landscape.

The naturalists and writers Ted Kerasote, Richard Nelson, and Barry Lopez at one time or another lived and hunted with the Inuit of the Arctic. The only American I'd ever heard of who had lived and hunted with Africans was the biologist and anthropologist Stuart Marks, whose book *Large Animals and a Brave People* explained the color categories of African animals. I first learned of Marks back in the 1970s when I read John Heminway's book *Imminent Rains,* in which he tells of the young couple he found living and doing graduate work in a Luangwa Valley village. Some time after that Marks came as a guest to our hunting lodge on the Savannah River, but nobody mentioned Heminway's book, and I failed to make the connection. When I returned from Africa I reread *Imminent Rains,* and it all came together.

A son of medical missionaries, Marks had grown up in what was then Zaire, where he first became interested in hunting traditions among Africans. He returned to the States for college and went on to do graduate work at Michigan State in wildlife ecology. During the summer of 1967, when I was moving to Athens, Georgia, to begin my academic career, Marks was doing Ph.D. research with the Valley Bisa at Nabwalya on the Luangwa River. That's where the young writer John Heminway found him. Heminway had recently finished at

Princeton and was driving from south-central Africa to Kenya, meeting and interviewing old survivors of the colonial days along the way. At Fort Jameson, Zambia, he heard of an American ecologist and his wife who were doing work in Nabwalya. As he tells it,

> There were no comforts in Nabwalya. Water had to be brought by hand from the river, one mile away. A bath was considered the supreme luxury. Their food was of the humblest variety. That which did not come out of tins was shot by Marks with his single-barreled shotgun given to him by the Game Department. For them there was little contact with other white people, as they had few visitors, and since they did not own a radio, no news from the outside world. Unlike most white people in Africa, they did their own housework and cooking as they believed the presence of a houseboy would have disrupted their study . . .
>
> Marks poaches with Africans. He does so with the blessing of the Game Department, which has promised him that if he is caught by one of the game guards he will immediately be released. Since poaching is the tribe's principal means of supplying themselves with food it is important for him to understand every aspect of it.

Large Mammals and a Brave People was the first result of Marks's work. In subsequent years he returned as often as possible to the Luangwa Valley, conducting research that led to the publication of *The Imperial Lion* in 1984. He was back in Nabwalya on a Fulbright in 1988 and has continued ever since to publish in professional journals his research on native hunting and big game.

When I read Marks's African books, they cast in retrospect a defining light upon my experience and colored my recollections. The big news was that there have always been hunters among the indigenous people of the Luangwa Valley.

CENTRAL AFRICA in ancient times was home to Bushmen, but around two thousand years ago Bantu tribes from the north began a slow, inexorable expansion that pushed the Bushmen south toward the lower end of the continent. The Luangwa Valley, bypassed by the

Bantu, remained uninhabited for many hundreds of years, but during the eighteenth century the Bantu tribes Chewa, Bemba, Bisa, and Kunda began a migration south from the Congo basin and settled in what is now eastern Zambia. Gradually, the stronger Bemba drove clans of Bisa from the plateau above the Muchinga Escarpment down into the agriculturally marginal country of the valley, where they established themselves in small villages along perennial streams, cultivating meager crops of sorghum and killing game with spears, snares, and pits. The Kunda meanwhile were drifting into country downstream from the Bisa. According to Kunda lore, they descended from Mambwe, a prince of the Luba empire, the only surviving son of a chief who had all of his male offspring put to death at birth. Like a young Moses, Mambwe survived to lead kinsmen of his mother's lineage down to the Luangwa, where in the early years of the nineteenth century they settled on the east bank at the confluence of that river with the Kauluzi. Exactly where we were hunting—the combretum plain where Steve had killed the puku, Stuart the impala, and I the kudu.

When David Livingstone encountered the Luangwa Valley tribes in December 1866, they had been brutalized by many years of Arab and Portuguese slave trade, which pitted tribe against tribe, village against village, and everyone against elephants, whose ivory was a major component of the slave-trade economy. The missionary-explorer came into the valley from the hills in the east, crossing country not far from Harry's fly camp, and followed the Lukuze River north toward the Luangwa. "The people," he wrote, "were all afraid of us, and we were mortified to find that food is scarce. The Mazitu [Zulu] have been here three times, and the fear they have inspired, though they were successfully repelled, has prevented agricultural operations from being carried on." Game, on the other hand, was abundant. Though he and his men grew tired of an exclusively meat diet, Livingstone shot "a fine male kudu," a "gnu," and a "pallah," for they could not buy grain "at any price."

Livingstone and his party crossed the swollen Luangwa not far below its confluence with the Lukuze, a point about forty miles upstream from our compound. The villages on the west bank, now the South Luangwa National Park, he called Babisa, though he stopped in the village of a chief named Kavimba, who appears from other sources to have been a grandson of the Kunda Mambwe. Whoever these Luangwa people were, Livingstone was not favorably impressed: "They have no more valor than the other Africans, but more craft, and are much given to falsehood. They will not answer common questions except by misstatements; but this may arise in our case from our being in disfavor, because we will not sell our goods to them for ivory."

In spite of the inhospitality of the people, Livingstone loved the valley. "I shall make this beautiful land better known," he wrote, "which is an essential part of the process by which it will become the 'pleasant haunts of men.' It is impossible to describe its rich luxuriance, but most of it is running to waste through the slave trade and internal wars."

The impression one gets of Luangwa tribesmen from reading Livingstone's journals is that of a desperate, half-starved people, living in wretched mud villages, their energy devoted entirely to defending themselves against the raids of the stronger Bemba, the fierce Ngoni, a branch of the Zulu, and half-caste Portuguese renegades. But Livingstone did not remain in any of these villages long enough to observe and understand their rituals and traditions. The culture of the valley tribes had developed around trade and their dependence on meat, which meant that hunting was a major activity of every village. Skilled hunters belonged to exclusive professional guilds that regulated all aspects of the hunt—who, when, where, what, and most significantly how. Only young men who had demonstrated sufficient bushcraft to kill large animals such as elephants and buffalo were admitted to membership. In many cases, the initiate had learned the rudiments of hunting from his mother's brothers, for these were matrilineal societies, and the bonds of matrikin constituted a strong institution. Because hunters were the distributors of meat for their clans and villages, membership in a guild was highly prestigious, and the power to kill elevated them to the status of an elite.

But going after elephant or buffalo with spear, bow, or even muzzle loader was a dangerous business. To propitiate ancestral spirits and to affect favorably the spiritual forces that haunted the bush, hunters observed elaborate sets of taboos and practiced arcane rituals, encoded by the traditions of their particular lineage. According to Marks's research, an elephant hunt might begin with guild members asking the chief for his blessing. He granted it by spitting on the hunters. The night before the hunt, each member of the party poured flour and a string of white beads into a gourd named for an ancestor and prayed for assistance. If the hunter dreamed favorably that night and found the gourd undisturbed the next morning, he would join the others, equipping himself with prescriptions or "magic" designed to increase chances of safety and success. It was also necessary that wives and kin who remained behind conduct themselves with propriety. If a woman committed adultery while her husband was gone, for example, she was placing him and the other members of the party in great danger. Mysteriously the elephants being hunted might sometimes gain knowledge of her domestic adventure and communicate the information to the hunter. In other words, the sight of elephants copulating might well abort the hunt and send the hunter quickly back to his village.

Only a small percentage of the men of a particular lineage became professional hunters. Nonguild members might hunt small game in the vicinity of their village, but the success of such individuals won no special recognition. The professionals, on the other hand, assumed great prestige as providers of ivory and distributors of meat. When one considers that hunting had such far-reaching political, economic, and even spiritual ramifications, it's easy to understand how the activity and its associated practices might organize a community and shape a culture.

During the last decade of the 1890s the British South Africa Company assumed administrative control of territory that would later become Northern and Southern Rhodesia, and with independence, Zambia and Zimbabwe. The laws the British imposed on the tribes of the Luangwa Valley, as elsewhere, altered native life. What Marks calls "the matrix of change" included the setting aside of tribal ancestral grounds as hunting reserves for Europeans, which restricted the tribes' freedom to move their villages from one place to another along the rivers and to hunt where they chose; registration of the large numbers of muzzle loaders that had become available for trade after the development of modern rifles; game laws that created boundaries, license fees, and bag limits; and taxation, which required males to seek employment in mines as far away as South Africa. Taxes, access by new roads to towns and cities, and the availability of muzzle loaders introduced a cash economy, which replaced the old barter system with its dependence on crafts and natural resources. Marks says, with scholarly understatement, "In their effects on Valley Bisa society, these changes have been more than the sum of their parts."

The hunting guilds died out soon after the British came, but the new regime did nothing to reduce the people's dependence on wild meat. Because of the tsetse fly, domestic animals could not survive in the valley, so if people were to consume animal protein, they would have to continue hunting, British laws or not. And they did, though now as individuals engaged in activity deemed illegal rather than as groups of proud professionals. For a long time many of these individuals managed to observe traditional patterns and rituals, but the generation that came of age at the time of independence, having been more widely exposed to modern urban life, abandoned the old ways, ignored the authority of the chief, lost touch with the lineage of matrikin as a primary cultural institution, and, if they hunted at all, used snares to catch animals that, if not needed for food, could be sold in city markets.

Independence did little to improve conditions for rural people, especially where hunting was concerned. Indoctrinated by European and American concepts of game management and conservation, Zambian government officials continued to treat wildlife as a national resource that could be marketed to the highest bidders—an international clientele of hunters and wildlife tourists—hardly taking into account the attitudes of tribesmen toward the large animals they lived among. In a particularly effective article, Marks juxtaposes in the persons of two men the opposing positions of "managerial ecology" and "lineage husbandry." His representative for the first of these is Sir Julian Huxley, who in 1960 was sent by UNESCO to study and report on the state of wildlife in East and Central Africa. Assuming an "original ecosystem" that "has suffered vast damages at the hands of man," Huxley insisted on the necessity for securing "the future of the habitat." Wildlife, he said, was "no longer merely a local matter," and he recommended "a bold official conservation policy based on scientific research, backed by world opinion and furnished with adequate finance."

The major threat to wildlife conservation in Africa, he reported, was poaching, which was increasing at an alarming rate and, if left unchecked, would soon wipe out entire animal populations. His solution was to change the attitudes of tribal Africans toward wildlife, make them understand that "organized game cropping can provide them with more and probably cheaper meat than organized poaching, and that illicit individual shooting is killing the goose that lays the golden eggs."

Until I went to Africa, Huxley's position made sense. Appalled by reports of commercial ivory poaching and the extermination of rhinos because of the value of their horns, I applauded Richard Leakey's drastic antipoaching measures in Kenya. *The End of the Game* by Peter Beard and *The Eye of the Elephant* by Mark and Delia Owens convinced me that Africans were the bad guys, ruthlessly destroying our Garden of Eden, and if poachers lost their lives while hacking out the tusks of elephants, too bad. At the very least, Africans should learn to eat domestic meat. But once I began to pay attention to the faces of the men who walked the dusty roads through the Lupande GMA, it occurred to me that Africans might have a story too. It is to be heard, I learned from Stuart Marks, in the tribal practices that make up what he calls "lineage husbandry."

Among local hunters in the Luangwa Valley, prescriptions for successfully overcoming failures of various kinds, interpretations of events, knowledge, awards, incentives, recognition of ancestral guidance, and affiliation within a social field all are expressed within a particular cultural framework. This framework, or paradigm, I call *lineage husbandry*. It is difficult, maybe impossible, to capture the essence or translate the meanings of *lineage husbandry* into English without undue slippage of contexts and without using a prejudicial vocabulary.

Instead of a definition Marks gives us an example in the person of a Bisa tribesman named Luben Kafupi, a man "Huxley would have readily dismissed as a 'poacher.'" Marks came to know Kafupi as a neighbor in Nabwalya in 1967–68. When Marks asked him why he hunted, Kafupi replied:

> My maternal grandfather, a great hunter, visited me in a dream telling me to find a gun and begin hunting. When I told my maternal uncle about this dream, he advised me to go and purchase a [muzzle-loading] gun in Serenje District. For this I used money earned while working in Wankie [then Southern Rhodesia]. When I returned, my uncle called all of our relatives together. Each elder in my lineage, there were three men and several women, put three white beads on a string and tied them around my gun. My maternal uncle as senior member of the lineage pronounced the following blessing: "Uwaice nyu akwate imfuti. Ayokwendo mutende muchonde. Ayokwipaya inama kulya palupwa." [This youngster now has a gun. May he be protected in the bush and kill animals so the lineage may eat.] Before dispersing, we put other white beads into a *nkombo* [a special gourd with a long handle and an opening for offerings] and it was named and dedicated to my late ancestor.

Kafupi's answer to Marks's question shows clearly that for him, as for many other tribesmen, hunting had to do with more than subsistence. Much more. It had to do with cultural identity, with a way of being in a landscape that was as much a spiritual as a physical reality, a way that had been forged through millennia of slowly changing interaction with creatures who assumed metaphysical significance. The

Valley Bisa that Marks came to know were not noble savages, but their ways of responding to their habitat were a vestige of the hunter-gatherers from whom they descended. When Marks returned to Nabwalya as a Fulbright Fellow in 1988–89, he found Kafupi too old to hunt, but in spite of radical changes in Bisa society and the wildlife of the Luangwa Valley during the intervening twenty-five years, the old man had managed to pass on to his sons, grandsons, and nephews the hunting traditions that he had inherited in his time.

ON A SUNDAY MORNING ten months after I returned from Zambia I sat talking with Stuart Marks in his condo in northern Virginia. For the last several years he has worked for Safari Club International as senior scientist for research and community development. His hair had begun to gray since I'd seen him last, but other than that he had changed little in twenty years. Still trim, he had the energy of a much younger man, and he was much engaged by Africa. As we talked, he picked up a long-necked gourd with a small hole in its belly and asked if I knew what it was. It was African, I could tell that, but all I could think of was a nest gourd for purple martins. I had to say no.

"This is an nkombo," Stuart said.

Ah. A hunter's ancestor, or a surrogate thereof.

"Are those still in use?" I asked.

"Not much."

Having read Stuart's books and many of his articles, I had a fair grasp of Bisa hunting through the late 1980s, when he went back to spend a year at Nabwalya, but what had been going on since then? What had been the effect of the commercial ivory poaching of the eighties? Had it been stopped? How extensive was meat poaching?

Careful scholar that he is, Stuart resisted easy answers and simplistic explanations. I could tell by the way he cleared his throat that the professor was arranging his lecture notes. I flipped to a clean sheet in my pad.

"It's hard to list changes and explain causes because everything is so interrelated. Every situation affects a dozen others and is affected in turn in a dozen different ways. But if you have to start somewhere, I guess ADMADE is a good place."

Harry Chapman had told Steve that forty percent of safari revenue is returned to the people who live in the area where we were hunting. The community-based wildlife management program that served as mechanism for the distribution of funds is called, in splendid bureaucratese, Administrative Management Design, or ADMADE.

"It looked good on paper," Stuart said. "Money from trophy fees and access fees to the park is returned to a sub-district management authority, which includes the chief and various civil servants, and they are supposed to spend it on what they call 'development,' schools and clinics and grinding mills, community projects. The idea is that locals will benefit from these improvements and come to see that it's in their interest to protect wildlife, even to the extent of reporting poachers. The problem is, in the first place, that very little of the money ever gets back to the sub-district. A study from 1992 showed only two percent."

"So it never gets out of Lusaka?"

Stuart spread his hands, palms out.

"And the people aren't helped at all?"

"The people have actually been hurt. ADMADE was supposed to provide cheap bushmeat as compensation for denying people access to hunting, but instead of making it available in local villages, the government has been selling it in the cities for its own profit."

"Then who is killing the animals?"

"Game guards, wildlife management people."

"The ones who are supposed to be protecting the game."

"They're protecting it for themselves. The presence of game enforcement in the valley has not stopped native hunting, it's just driven it underground. People are using snares now more than ever because they don't make noise, which means among other things that you don't have to be a hunter anymore to take game. When hunting was managed by local elders, young men had to go through a tutelage. By controlling access to the lineage gun, which was a muzzle loader, the elders controlled who hunted at any given time. No more than twenty-five percent of the men of any village were approved hunters. But now anybody can set snares."

Stuart got up and walked over to a file cabinet. "Listen to this," he said. Retrieving an offprint of an article, he continued, "This is what a village elder told me just a few years ago." Flipping pages and finding the place, he read: "'My uncle taught me both to hunt with a gun and with wire snares, just in case the situation changed as it has today with many game guards. Their presence, which prevents us from pursuing game, is contrary to the wishes of our ancestors. This is a bad situation. Our ancestors settled in this country of wild animals, killed, and fed upon game, yet the animals never decreased. That's why our sons and grandsons have got on with what their fathers and forefathers used to do. Outside people tell us, "you have finished the animals." Now I ask you, how can a muzzle-loading gun finish animals when it fires only once in comparison with semi-automatic rifles? Rather, those who have come from outside for business are the ones who have diminished our animals.'"

"Do you have an extra copy of that?" I asked.

Stuart handed the offprint to me. "A Century of Change in the Central Luangwa Valley of Zambia," by Joel Freehling and Stuart A. Marks.

"That appeared in a collection called *Conservation of Biological Resources.* 1998."

I thumbed through it, stopping at a section entitled "Trends in wildlife numbers." A graph showed population fluctuations of eight major species in the valley from 1890 to 1990. Except for wildebeest and zebra, every species had declined from a high in the 1960s. The rhino of course was gone.

"Elephants have begun to recover somewhat in the last ten years, but almost everything else is in decline, as much as fifty percent for many species."

"And the cause?"

"A combination of things—years of drought, poor national economy, population growth in the valley, wildlife commercialization, and everything that's meant by 'poaching.' Too many people killing animals. Natives, game guards, wildlife officials."

"What about safari hunting? Aren't those the people who come from outside for business?"

"No, those are the commercial poaching rings. The effect of safari hunting is negligible. In fact, the safari presence tends to discourage illegal hunting, and I don't say that because it pays my bills, but it's probably not as effective as the safari people would like to believe."

I HAD TOLD Stuart about the kudu, recounting the story with the pride I would take in hanging the mounted head on a wall, but I had not mentioned the killing of the puku. Now it seemed necessary. "The day I killed the kudu," I began, "I shot a puku too. Unofficial. Unrecorded. Unreported. We were driving through the bush, across the combretum plain where I shot the kudu, and suddenly Harry stopped. I thought he needed to take a leak or something, but he turned to me and asked if I wanted to shoot a puku. A buck and a couple of does were grazing maybe a hundred yards out to the left. The whole thing took me by surprise. I mean, it didn't make sense. But nobody else seemed to question it. It was like I was the only one who didn't understand what was going on, and nobody bothered to explain. It was a matter of either do it or ask why, so I took the rifle and started over the side, but Harry said, 'No, just go ahead and pop him from there.' I didn't much want to shoot the animal in the first place and especially not from the vehicle, but whatever was going on was not the kind of situation in which such reservations mattered. At least not to anybody else. So I shot and the puku went down, but I made a bad shot and crippled it, and the trackers had to chase it down and cut its throat. I felt pretty sick about it, but Harry explained, after the fact, that the game scout had requested meat. There was no meat in the game scout village, and Mbuluma had told Harry that if we could shoot an animal for him, he wouldn't report it. I guess that made me feel a little better, but I still had the feeling that I had been given a nasty job. Whatever it was, it wasn't hunting. It didn't have anything to do with hunting.

"In one of your books you describe the four stages of the hunt—scanning, stalking, shooting, and retrieval. If I had been able to participate in any one of those, it might have been different, but I wasn't. We were standing there looking at the dead puku, and Harry said that because of the circumstances we couldn't take the horns or the skin. I thought, 'Who cares?'"

Maybe I was hoping that Stuart would respond to the story with an observation that might throw a different light on what I had done, but all he said was, "So you're a poacher? Right?" Then he smiled.

What he was telling me, I realized after I left, was that I had gotten to participate in the native hunting experience as it is today, illegal, underground, invisible. Much of what I had learned in reading his work and talking with him during the weekend I had already experienced firsthand. The trackers had spotted the puku, the vehicle had "stalked" it, Karim had cut its throat, and Mbuluma had brought it in. The whole process was bleakly utilitarian—no ritual, no ceremony, no celebration—it was bushmeat poaching, the condition to which native hunting in the Luangwa Valley has been reduced.

Getting to stalk and shoot the kudu thirty minutes later could not have been mere coincidence, any more than the similarities of the names of the animals are. Compare the words *puku* and *kudu*. Both are Bantu derivatives, both name an antelope, both sound the same vowels in the same order. But think how much more noble "kudu" sounds to us than "puku."

▼ ▼ ▼

Two DAYS before the end of the safari, we came upon the lion again, the black-maned lion that had roared behind the blind. We were making a routine check at the same bait in the middle of the morning, and as the vehicle approached the tree where the bait hung, the lion rose from the grass and walked off, unhurried, into the bush. Harry followed him for maybe a hundred yards in the vehicle, and for that brief space Steve could have taken a rifle shot. I doubt that such a thing even occurred to him, but Harry told me later that the trackers were "bitter" over Steve's refusal to take advantage of the opportunity. I thought "bitter" was too strong a word, but they were disappointed. A lion kill is for them an occasion for an all-night party. The client is obliged by custom to give the staff cigarettes, enough beer to last until daylight, and large tips; they dance themselves into exhaustion and get to sleep it off the next morning. I had been hoping from the start to witness that celebration.

Harry ordered a *machan* built. He was planning to stay all night, and a ground blind is too risky for that. Mbuluma dismantled the old blind where we had waited for the lion the week before, and Silas and Demetrius cut and trimmed long, sturdy poles. Three of these with the trunk of a living tree would serve as the foundation posts. I watched fascinated as the two trackers scampered up and down the poles, laid a flimsy platform, and enclosed it with walls of bundled grass.

After a while Karim came over to the shade where I was sitting and took a soda from the ice chest. Ever since our campfire discussion of religious faith, I had wondered about his knowledge of the Twenty-third Psalm. This seemed a good time to ask.

He smiled. "I was brought up Catholic. My mother is Catholic. I attended a Catholic school."

"And later converted to Islam?"

"Yes, but only after long study. My father's faith had a great influence, but I honor both religions."

"You asked me the other night what being a Christian meant to me. Let me ask you the same thing. Why did you choose Islam?"

"Because of the five pillars. There is but one God. Allah is His name and Muhammad is His prophet. That pillar is like the tree that supports the *machan*. There are four more that tell us how we must live: we must pray five times every day, we must fast during Ramadan, we must give alms to the poor, and we must make hajj to Mecca at least once in our lives. Each is important, but they all depend on the strength of the first. The *machan* would not stand apart from the tree. Do you understand?"

The building of the *machan* took two hours. When it was finished, we returned to camp for lunch and a short nap. Harry wanted us to be ready to return at 3:00. He made that clear. At 2:55 we were seated in the Land Cruiser, waiting for Silas and Demetrius. They had loaded the back with rolled mattresses and filled the cooler, but they must have returned to their huts for last minute matters. At 3:00 Harry blew the horn, which was answered by a shout from behind the wall of the kitchen compound. Two minutes later Harry tooted the horn again. Again came a shout. Harry shifted into low and drove through the gate. No one said a word. A half-mile down the road he stopped. "Do we have the kudu?" he asked.

Harry was planning to hang a hindquarter for bait and to use the kudu viscera in spreading scent around the site.

Karim looked around toward the back and said, "No."

Harry jammed the shifter into reverse, backed around, and headed toward camp, driving too fast for the condition of the road. As we approached the gate, Silas and Demetrius came running from behind the wall, Silas carrying the hindquarter across the back of his shoulders, Demetrius holding the guts in both hands.

Harry turned toward us seated on the bench, and speaking quite calmly, said, "I'm going to have to ask you to forgive me for this." Facing the trackers, he unleashed his anger. The words were Nyanja, his tone scathing. Silas, looking at his feet, mumbled a response, but Harry lashed back, "No excusi!"

I was unable to tell whether the confrontation was racial or simply a matter of the boss man bawling out a worker, but in that role Harry was clearly the master and the trackers black servants. If they resented the reprimand, they showed no sign that they did but climbed meekly into the back of the vehicle, making room for themselves and the kudu parts amongst the mattresses.

AT THE BAIT TREE, Silas undertook the hanging of the kudu hindquarter, hoisting it by cable alongside the shroud of hippo hide, and over at the *machan* Mbuluma began handing bedding up to Karim. Demetrius, meanwhile, tied a length of twine around the guts, punched a hole in one of the stomachs, and began to slap that vile ropy package against the tree where the bait was hanging. The odor would carry a long way on the night breezes, reminding the lion who smelled it that supper was served. Supervising the preparations,

Harry got too close to the action, and when Demetrius slung the guts a daub of the contents splatted Harry in the face. Instead of exploding in anger, as I expected, he smiled and shook his finger at the tracker, saying something in Nyanja. Demetrius smiled in return but said nothing. Harry soaked his handkerchief with water from the jerry can in the vehicle and washed his face.

When Steve, Harry, and Stuart had climbed into the *machan,* the rest of us bade them a noisy good-bye, hoping any lion that might be watching would think the whole crew had left. A mile or so back along the track we'd come in on, Karim pulled off into an open grove of trees on the left. "We'll camp here tonight," he said. The trackers and Mbuluma immediately set about gathering wood, but instead of laying one big fire they prepared three small ones, the points of an equilateral triangle about twenty feet apart. Then they dragged a log over to form one side of the triangle, and there we sat, eating our supper sandwiches.

Being alone with Africans as the sun went down made me conscious not so much of my skin, which in any case was no longer white, at least where it showed, as of my foreignness, but that was not the only thing that separated me from my companions, who etymologically speaking are those who share bread together. I was old enough to be a father of each one of them. In their eyes I was the old man, the graybeard from America who could not speak Nyanja. For almost three weeks we had been together daily but always in prescribed roles. What did I know of their histories, their beliefs, their families? No more than they knew of mine. We all had stories but how were we to tell them to each other?

Maybe through Karim the translator, speaker of native tongues, devotee of two faiths, vessel of black, brown, and white blood, the true African.

AT DARK they lit the fires. As the flames quickened, creatures began to stir all around us, making calls I couldn't identify, but amidst the strange sounds, I recognized the rising whoops of hyenas, which reminded me of stories I had read and heard of hyenas biting off the faces of people sleeping in the bush. I asked Karim if they really did that. He translated the question, and the black men responded with soft laughter. Demetrius said something, and Karim passed it on to me. "Demetrius says, 'That's why we put you in the middle tonight.'" Karim pointed to the space within the triangle of campfires. "You will sleep there." Even as he spoke, Demetrius was fetching the one remaining mattress and pillow from the back of the Land Cruiser.

Special treatment was my right as a client, bought and paid for, but tonight I wanted to be one of the boys. "What about y'all?" I asked.

"We will get our rest," Karim said.

THIS WAS THE NIGHT of the full moon. Every night so far I had watched it come up over the Luangwa, later and later, rounder and rounder. Now I lay back on the mattress as it rose upon our campsite, magnified and yellow. A tree growing on the bank of the dry bed of the Kauluzi River stood between the moon and me, its horizontal branches forming the rungs of a ladder, and I marked the passing of time by the moon's ascent from branch to branch. Before it cleared the top it went behind a cloud cover, backlighting the thick flannel that spread across the dome of the sky, and the night grew darker. Karim and the trackers were talking quietly—talking about lions, I suspected—but whatever the topic of their measured conversation, the soft murmur of their voices brought me peace.

When I awoke, our campsite was silvered in moonlight. A strong wind aloft had tugged open a ragged hole in the cloud cover, and there shone the moon in full splendor, as bright as it was meant to be, and revealing the faces of the Africans. Karim and Mbuluma and Silas were leaning back against the log, and Demetrius was stretched out full length on the ground, but it seems to me now that another man whose face I cannot see had joined the party. By the position of the moon, I judged that I must have dozed for an hour.

"Listen, Doc," Karim said when he saw that I was awake. "The lion has been roaring from the park. He's moving in this direction."

MY MEMORY of that evening is bathed in the moonlight that dreams are made of, but the murmur of real voices telling true stories in another tongue gives ballast to the dream. Demetrius speaks, and Silas and Mbuluma in their turn; the stranger, a Bisa tribesman named Lubeles, through the voice of Stuart Marks, tells about the killing of an elephant, and though I do not hear among these accents the Scottish burr of old David Livingstone, I can tell he's around.

I get up from the mattress and sit on the cooler, facing the Africans. The small fire at my back feels good in the chill of the moonlight.

Silas speaks; Karim translates: "Bwana Harry won't need to use the spotlight tonight. They can see by the moon."

"Will the lion come before morning?"

"Yes, the lion will come," Demetrius says. "Bwana Harry's heart is good."

Silas and Mbuluma laugh. Karim explains. "They believe that if the hunter has a bad heart, game won't come. The animals can tell, and they will stay away. When Harry got angry this afternoon, his heart went bad, but Demetrius made him laugh when he slung the guts, and the laughter cleansed Harry's heart. Now the lion will come."

Silas says something, and the others chuckle softly to themselves. "Silas says that Demetrius is not telling all of the truth. He says that when Harry yelled at them this afternoon in front of everybody he put shit on them so Demetrius slung the guts and put shit back on Harry."

"But it worked, didn't it? I mean, Harry did laugh."

"Yes," Karim says, "both things are true."

THE LANGUAGE BARRIER has discouraged me from asking these men about their lives—their families, their beliefs, their experiences as hunters—but the deeper reason has been a reluctance to encroach upon their privacy. Now Karim reminds me that I have wanted to hear their stories. This is a good time, he says.

Demetrius the tracker, blessed with eagle's eyes, wears a quilted jacket, once red but faded now to pink. He is of the Kaonde tribe from northwestern Zambia, a handsome man, lean and of medium height, and the color of his skin is a richer, warmer chocolate than I have seen among the Kunda. His father was a game guard, he says, but as a young man he made a living as a hunter, poaching for bushmeat and selling it on the black market. When he moved to his father's village, his father explained to him the dangers of poaching—going to jail or even getting shot—and persuaded him to quit. So he took a job with the department of roads. "After a short time, I was operating a pontoon bridge. That job I held for twelve years, until Chiluba came in. The new government cut back on jobs, and I had nothing to do. I returned to my home and soon I heard that a safari company in my area was hiring people. I applied for a position as a general worker. One day one of the trackers got sick and the PH took me out in his place. God blessed me with the eyes of the eagle. I saw a red hartebeest that no one else could see, and I led the client to a place where he could shoot. The client was a rich man from Spain, and he was shooting a fine and expensive rifle. He wounded the hartebeest and I tracked it for a great distance, several hours. When we found it, it proved to be a trophy. The client was very happy."

Karim's translation sounds stilted and formal, as though he is carefully picking key words from the rich broth of Demetrius's talk.

"The PH returned to bring the vehicle, and I took the fine rifle and laid it aside, in a safe place, but when the PH drove up he ran over it and cracked it. He was very angry with me, but the client didn't care because of the hartebeest I had found for him. For the rest of that safari he asked the PH to bring me on the hunt. In that way the PH came to see that I had keen eyesight so he made me an apprentice tracker. When Bwana Harry came to work for that company, I became his tracker. I have stayed with him ever since. We go to Tanzania, we go to Zimbabwe; we come here to this camp. All I know of tracking I have learned from Bwana Harry. I am very happy with him."

"Do you have a family?" I ask.

"Yes, my wife and I we have five children but only two are living."

I start to speak, to express sympathy for such unimaginable loss, but Karim says, "Shh. Listen."

The night is alive with sounds, but the roar of the lion, though faint and far away to the north, disperses the louder calls of lesser creatures and resonates from the center of the darkness. "Mbulumu," Karim says.

The scout doesn't respond, but Karim explains to me: "Mbulumu. In their language it means the roar of a lion."

"WHAT DOES IT TAKE to be a great tracker or hunter, besides good eyesight?" I ask Demetrius.

"You must be alert in the bush at all times, never forget, because you do not know what the bush will bring. And your wife, she must behave herself while you are gone."

Silas and even Mbuluma laugh softly, showing their teeth.

"And she must eagerly want you to return. Her longing for you will keep you safe because it draws you back to her."

SILAS the poacher goes barefooted in the bush. At the beginning of the safari we invited the members of the staff to pick out shoes for themselves. Silas chose a pair of Adidas but unlike the others he has not worn his. Yet he takes them with him wherever he goes. When Harry asked him why, he said, "Never again will I own such shoes as these. Why should I use them up in the bush?"

"Then why do you bring them on the hunt?" Harry asked.

Silas did not answer, but Harry told us later that Silas was afraid to let them out of his sight, someone would surely steal them.

Silas has the guilty look of a thief himself, long-limbed, loose-jointed, shuffling and shy. He averts his eyes when spoken to, and he never initiates conversation as Demetrius does. While working on the *machan,* he clung to the crosspieces as much with his feet as with his hands, as though his toes were prehensile. And when a bait was hung, it was Silas who climbed the tree, clasping the trunk with those tough feet, then standing on the bulk of rotted meat, tightening the knot.

"I was a poacher," he says. "That is how I learned the bush. I hunted for ivory and for bushmeat."

Oh, I think, so I am talking face to face with one of the bad guys in *The Eye of the Elephant.*

Mark and Delia Owens's book recounts their fight against ivory poaching in the North Luangwa Park. At the time of their arrival in the late eighties, they estimated that over the previous fifteen years, seventy-five thousand or more elephants had been slain by commercial poachers—a rate of kill that would soon wipe out the population, as poaching had extirpated black rhinos in the Luangwa Valley. At first, the Owenses turned to game scouts for help, but they quickly learned that nearly everyone, from scouts to wardens to high government officials in Lusaka, were participating in the illegal ivory trade. Next, they sought to establish cottage industries in surrounding villages, believing that once the people learned to generate income by legitimate means they would no longer need to work for the poachers. When those efforts failed, Mark Owens declared war. Detecting poachers from the air and harassing them with his Cessna, he succeeded in restricting their activities, but as of 1992 when the book was published poaching was still a problem in the Luangwa Valley.

By his own account, Owens conducted his war against poaching at great personal risk, reminding the reader of such martyrs to the cause of conservation as Dian Fossey in Rwanda and George Adamson in Kenya. On one occasion, when poachers fire into the thatch huts of men who have worked with him, Owens says that sooner or later someone is going to be killed. "Clearly, they are upping the ante. If they can do it, so can I." He begins to speak of the poachers as "the enemy" and the North Park as a "war zone." He flies antipoaching patrols night and day, sleeping little and surviving on coffee. Delia, concerned about his growing obsession, tells him, "you've crossed over the line," but Mark refuses to ease up.

When the Chiluba administration takes over, Owens receives at last the help he has needed, especially a contingent of trained and well-equipped game scouts who are willing to go out on patrol. His instructions to them as they prepare on one occasion to go in pursuit: "If you come across the poachers, don't wait for them to shoot first." At this point in the narrative the reader wants to stand up and clap. The bad guys are about to get what's coming to them. But who were these bad guys? According to the Owenses, they were a ring of five ruthless men of the Bemba tribe who recruited local hunters, armed them with AK-47s, and sent them into the park to slaughter elephants. But Stuart Marks, who was living in Nabwalya at that time, says that they were also poor villagers like Silas.

In the flicker of the campfire, I ask Silas if he has ever heard of Mark Owens.

"Oh," he says, "Mark Owens was a fierce man. He would come in his airplane or his helicopter and terrorize poachers. He always found them. They could not get away."

I wonder how closely I dare question Silas. "Did you ever know any of the people who hunted ivory in the North Park?"

"Yes."

"Did they make a lot of money?"

Silas smiles. "The people outside, the big people, they are the ones who make the money."

"What caused you to stop poaching and come to work for the safari?"

"I was afraid."

"Afraid of getting caught?"

"I was afraid of Mark Owens and his men. You know him, this man Mark Owens?"

"No, but I read a book that he and his wife wrote about elephant poaching in the North Park. It is called *The Eye of the Elephant*. Have you heard of it?"

"I am told that many people come here to the Luangwa and write books about us and about the animals, but these books we do not see, nor do we get money from them."

David Livingstone, Denis Lyell, Owen Letcher, Peter Capstick, Norman Carr, Stuart Marks, Mark and Delia Owens. A long record of hunting the Luangwa Valley, in one way or another—different times, different experiences, different attitudes, but all white. Yet I am unaware of any book written about the Luangwa by a native African. Does Silas feel used or is he frustrated by the impossibility of telling his own story? He has a story, for he has been out among large animals.

Not long ago I told my three-year-old granddaughter about the time my friend Jeff Carter touched a deer in a cane thicket, and she said, "Tell me the other side, Papa." I'm still not sure I understand what she meant by that, but I know there's another side to Silas's story, a side different from that told in *The Eye of the Elephant,* in which he appears as an unnamed, faceless poacher running from Mark Owens's airplane. But how is he to tell it?

My impulse is to tell it for him. Taking what I have learned from Stuart Marks and from the work of Mark and Delia Owens and coloring that with my sensory impressions of this valley, I could set Silas to talking right now, as he sits here amid these fires in the moonlight, and I believe the story would be his own. But it wouldn't be as true as his tough feet climbing trees or creeping through the bush.

MBULUMA the game scout, whose face presents an ebony mask, is such a proud man, hardly ever entering into the camaraderie between the trackers, that I am reluctant to ask him to talk about himself, but when Karim asks if I want to hear what Mbuluma has to say, I say yes, I sure do.

Like Silas, the game scout is Kunda, a native of the Mfuwe area. For all I know he may be kin to Silas. Although he lives in the Milyoti Gate village with the other scouts and their families, his wife stays in Mfuwe so their children can go to school. Mbuluma places great value on education. Instead of turning to poaching as Silas did, he found work with an American wildlife biologist named Dale Lewis, from whom he learned the techniques of darting animals, equipping them with radios, and tracking the signals. He became a wildlife technician, which may be why he appears to hold himself above the trackers. Yet when there is work to be done, dragging an animal or cutting brush for a *machan,* Mbuluma, though not paid by the safari company, is too proud to sit in the shade while others sweat.

The change of administrations, which brought Chiluba to the presidency and cost Demetrius his job at the pontoon bridge, made Mbuluma a game scout. When Lewis's project was completed, the new parks department kept his technicians and trained them to work as game guards. Mbuluma's job involves monitoring safaris and reporting kills, accompanying walking safaris in the park, and going out on antipoaching patrols. His equipment consists of an olive green uniform, combat boots, and the battered old rifle, .300 caliber, with welded-on iron sights. Harry told us that he probably had no more than five bullets—not much protection against the AK-47s of the commercial poachers.

Fortunately the commercial ivory-poaching rings have been broken up, thanks in part to the Owenses and to individuals such as Norman Carr but mainly to the international ban on ivory trade, which Zambia signed onto when Chiluba became president.

"Is poaching still a problem?" I ask Mbuluma.

"Yes," he says, "but now for meat only. Very little for ivory."

"Do they use snares or guns?"

"They use both but mostly snares."

"How do you find them in such a large area as the South Park and the Lupande?"

"We scout for their tracks, or we spot their fires at night, and sometimes people tell us where the poachers go. We know the country too. We are better hunters."

"Better than Silas?"

Silas laughs softly, and Mbuluma smiles, showing strong white teeth. "We never caught Silas. He was too fast. But we shot at him often."

"You shot at Silas? You yourself?"

"Twenty-three times they shoot at me," Silas says, and I see his smile too. "Sometimes Mbuluma, I think. But they never catch me. I run too fast for Mbuluma."

Mbuluma says something that Karim does not translate.

"Do you catch many?" I ask.

"Yes, more now."

"Why is that?"

"Because we are better equipped and we try harder."

"What happens when they're caught?"

"They go to jail. For a long time if they are repeaters."

"These poachers are Kunda like yourself. What happens if you catch a cousin or an uncle?"

"I cannot treat him differently from the others."

I am reminded of what the Bisa elder said about game guards to Stuart Marks: "Their presence, which prevents us from pursuing game, is contrary to the wishes of our ancestors. This is a bad situation. Our ancestors settled in this country of wild animals, killed, and fed upon game."

"Let me tell you about Lubeles," says Stuart Marks. And there he is, sitting across from me, between Karim and Demetrius, just as he was in his apartment outside of Washington, leaning forward, his elbows on his knees, and he holds an *nkombo* in his hand.

"When I was in Nabwalya the first time, back in '66 and '67, I was granted a director's permit to kill an elephant, which was legal in those days before the commercial poaching. My plan was to offer the permit to some hunter in exchange for his letting me go along on the hunt with him. I didn't want to shoot an elephant myself, but I was anxious to observe the Bisa style of hunting and the traditional rituals associated with the kill."

Yes, Stuart Marks, fellow academic, observer, notetaker, I understand.

"Lubeles was the natural choice. He was a young man, just a few years older than I. He had already accompanied me on several hunts, serving as a guide, and I paid him by dividing meat with him. We got along well together. But before I get to the elephant hunt, you need to hear Lubeles's story.

"He grew up in the valley village of Chibulu, heir to a lineage of hunters. When he was six, a maternal uncle made him a bow and arrows, and with that he learned to stalk and kill guineas and francolins around the village. When he was in his early teens, his father, a headman named Chando, gave him a larger bow and taught him to hunt impala. Before long he had killed six, establishing himself as a competent hunter and within his lineage a distributor of meat.

"He got married when he was seventeen and moved to a city in the Copperbelt, where he found a job as a guard on an underground train, but two years later he was back in Chibulu. He obtained from his lineage the prescription for chilembe, which is a magic rubbed into cuts in the hunter's wrist so that its effects might pass through the gun to the bullet and cause the animal's blood to clot inside its chest. Lubeles's wife made two incisions in his right wrist, and the magic entered his veins. He was now a hunter. The headman of the village, who was a cousin of Lubeles, had purchased an old muzzle loader, and since he didn't hunt himself, Lubeles had the use of it. His father Chando taught him how to stalk and kill buffalo. When he killed his first one, he gave a great feast—the vizemba ceremony—and his wife prepared beer and porridge.

"After a couple of years that wife died. Lubeles remarried and returned to the Copperbelt. He was then twenty-four. He got a job crushing rock underground and later as a concentrator, but he just couldn't stand the city. He missed the bush and the life of a hunter. So three years later he returned to Chibulu and devoted himself to hunting full time. He told me that he used to kill three or four buffalo a year, in addition to impala, warthog, and puku. When Luangwa Safaris came to the valley, Lubeles got a job with them as a tracker. He had two wives now and needed the added income. But safari work suited him. He enjoyed going out with Americans and Europeans and he especially liked handling their rifles. The clients were also good tippers. If Lubeles spotted a good trophy and the client was successful, he would do well.

"It was at this time that I first met him. The safari season was over and he had returned to Chibulu, and he started going out with me. He expected to be paid, of course, but I was not in a position financially to give him anything but a portion of the meat I killed. He agreed to that, and we became friends. Since he had never killed an elephant himself, which the Bisa call 'the mother of all mammals,' I figured he would jump at the chance to use my permit. And he did. There would be great prestige in it for him if he were successful.

"Usually, Lubeles hunted with that borrowed muzzle loader, and that's what he was planning to take, but since this was elephant we were hunting I arranged for him to use the chief's rifle—a

.375 magnum like my own, which I took along as a backup. We hunted for eight days, dawn to dark, and we saw a good many elephants, but we never could get within range of a big bull.

"When we came in that night after the eighth day, Lubeles told his parents about our lack of success. Neither of us had a bad heart, as your professional hunter did after yelling at the trackers, and we had not had intercourse with our wives, which, according to the Bisa, is associated with the village and the hearth, which are considered 'hot' and out of tune with the bush, which is 'cold.' Lubeles and I were not 'hot,' but apparently he had not prayed adequately for the approval of the ancestral spirits that inhabit the bush and draw near the edge of the village at nightfall. So Chando, Lubeles's father, had us sit in a circle in front of their hut, and then he prayed: 'You our ancestors go before us we pray. And you BaChiluba we pray go before us. Let there be luck.' Lubeles's grandfather Chiluba was considered an especially effective aid because he himself had been a great hunter. The next morning Lubeles told me that today we would kill an elephant."

I am reminded of the Banyai elephant hunter who said to David Livingstone, "I see you are traveling with people who don't know how to pray."

"And sure enough," Stuart continues, "late that morning we came upon a mature bull. He was by himself, dozing in a thin stand of winter acacia. We stalked to within twenty-five yards, and Lubeles had a good broadside shot at the heart. When he fired, the bull ran, but I managed a snap shot and hit him in the head. Lubeles took off in pursuit, and I followed. We came upon him standing in some trees, and Lubeles fired. This time the elephant fell, but then got to its feet, and Lubeles shot again, and again the elephant went down, but almost immediately was on its feet and running. Lubeles got off one more shot, which missed, and that was his last bullet, but he took off after the bull anyway. When I caught up with him, the elephant was standing with its back to us maybe fifty yards away. It was up to me then. My first shot hit him in the back and brought him down, but even then he tried to get up again. I finished it with a shot to the head."

The lion roars out of the north, still distant from us but closer to the bait—the same sound heard by Livingstone in these same mopani woods a hundred and forty years earlier—and the roar evokes the man, silent and dour but present even so, moving around the perimeter of our fires, attending to his legacy—Kunda Silas with his Christian name, a Roman Catholic; Demetrius an Apostolic; Mbuluma, who learned to read and write in a mission school; Karim Abdul-Hassan, a native of Livingstone, Zambia, whose slave trading Arab-Swahili ancestors could have traveled with the missionary; and my friend Stuart Marks, who grew up in Zaire because his parents were missionaries.

"I was eager to examine the elephant's tusks," Stuart continues, "but Lubeles wouldn't let me approach the carcass. He believed, as he had been taught, that the spirit of fallen game—what they call chibanda—will enter the head of the hunter who has killed it and cause trouble if he approaches it without the right prescription for protection. 'If the animal's spirit is not placated,' Lubeles said, 'a hunter may wake up in the night screaming and shouting and will say that the chibanda has come and he will feel very sick and perspire.' I was really surprised that it had taken so many shots—well-placed shots too—to kill the bull, but as we walked back to the village Lubeles explained that the first of a species a hunter shoots is always hard to kill. The second will be easier because once they perform the vizemba ceremony and return the chibanda to the bush, the spirit of the one already slain will call others to the hunter.

"We found Chando sitting under a tree with another headman making a mat. Lubeles asked permission for us to join them. Once we were settled, Lubeles waited for his father to speak. After a while, Chando casually mentioned that he had heard seven shots. Bisa hunters discuss their experiences only among themselves, so Lubeles said that he needed to talk privately with his father. Chando asked his companion to excuse him, please, he had other work to do. It was not until we were on our way to Chando's place, well out of the hearing of anyone else, that Lubeles told his father that we had killed a big elephant. Chando wanted to know if we had approached it after it was dead, and Lubeles said no. And then he asked his father if he might do the vizemba ceremony, a ritual by which a hunter expresses gratitude to the ancestors for his success.

"Before we returned to the kill, Chando collected roots, and then along the way he gathered bark from a certain kind of tree. These were 'magic.' Mixed together, they would prevent the spirit of the elephant from entering the hunter. When we had approached to within fifty yards, Chando stopped us, crushed the roots and bark, gave a portion to Lubeles and a portion to me, and told us to chew but not to swallow. Then Chando had us close our eyes. That way, the spirit of the elephant wouldn't be able to see us. Chando then led us by a circuitous route to the carcass. With our eyes still shut, he placed our hands on the elephant's trunk and told us to spit into it. Next, he led us around to the other end of the animal and told us to spit into the anus, which is the second of the two orifices through which the chibanda might escape. Once we had done that, we could open our eyes. Lubeles ran his rifle through the elephant's hind legs, along its belly, and between its front legs. Then he climbed up onto the carcass and struck it in the ribs with the butt of the rifle. 'We nama tuli nenu,' he said, which means, 'You animal, we are with you.' Some lineages or traditions say 'You animal, it is not I who has killed you. It is God. Don't follow me.' After Lubeles had done that, Chando had me do the same thing. Then Chando tied a knot in one of the hairs of the tail, and the ritual was concluded. I took out my camera and asked if I might photograph Lubeles reenacting various phases of the procedure. Chando said I could.

"We cut off the tail and trunk and took them back to Chando's village. As we walked, Lubeles with that heavy trunk draped across his shoulders, he and his father discussed the distribution of the meat. The problem was that the elephant had been killed near several small villages, and those people would want a share, but Lubeles and Chando wanted to keep the meat for their own village. So Chando decided that I should make a speech claiming to have killed this elephant myself and say that I wanted to give the meat to people who had helped me with my research. If others wanted meat, they would have to help transport it back to Chando's village. I agreed to that, hoping to prevent a fight. At worst, it was still half true.

"Sure enough, when we returned to the carcass early next morning, a large crowd had already gathered. They said they had had to run off four lions, and you could see that the lions had broken into the stomach. As cuts of meat were removed, they were placed on pieces of skin for transport. It was hot and bloody work. Smelly too. Lubeles's mother and sister took meat from the head and set it aside for the vizemba ceremony. Another pile was reserved for the chief because Lubeles had used the chief's rifle. When the carcass had been reduced to a skeleton, Chando gave knives to three old widows to cut off whatever pieces might remain. They were notorious beggars, those three, always showing up at kills because they had no hunter to provide for them, and people ridiculed them when they went to work on the skeleton because cutting meat is not women's work, but they had tough hides too and paid no attention."

I DON'T KNOW if Demetrius, Silas, or Mbuluma have ever killed an elephant—Silas must have been in on killings—but all three have been nodding their heads and murmuring throughout Stuart's story, as though these things are familiar to them.

"WHILE THE CARCASS was being butchered, two or three men were busy chopping out the tusks, which is no small task. It took them four hours. When they had finished, two of the men took the tusks away while the women and the young men turned their faces. The Bisa believe that the pulp inside the tusk resembles a limp penis. Just the sight of it can make young men impotent and women barren. Even older men must protect themselves by chewing the leaves of a certain tree, which Chando had been gathering while the others were axing the tusks from the head. When they had carried them aside, the men spit leaf juice on the pulp and then heated the tusks over a fire. At a certain point they tapped the tusk and the pulp fell out. Then they burned it, lest some evil person come upon it later and use it in witchcraft against others.

"After we distributed meat among the people who had helped, Lubeles took a pile of elephant dung to the place where he had first wounded the elephant and flattened it on the ground with his feet. Lubeles called this kusidika chibanda, neutralizing the spirit of the elephant.

"A couple of days later they held the vizemba, not in Chibulu where Lubeles lived but in his father's village where he had been staying when we killed the elephant. In preparation Lubeles took bark from two kinds of trees, musangu, which is an acacia, and something called malenje. He then made little bundles of the acacia bark and tied them with the malenje roots and placed the bundles in the auricular canals of the elephant's skull. That was to prevent the next elephant he hunted from hearing him. Then he spent the rest of the afternoon buying beer and collecting poles to support the pot in which they planned to cook the head meat.

"I got there about six that evening with the chief's rifle. A pot of meat was simmering over one fire, and some of the women were cooking nsima over another. Most of the people were sitting around the fire where the meat was cooking, the men on the west side, the women on the east, and a space for dancing was left open between them.

"I wish you could have seen the way they danced. It started with the men leading the women in a chant. They would sing a line, deep bass, and then the sweet soprano echo, and then the clapping, which established the rhythm for the dance. Lubeles got up and began to dance in the clear space. Soon he was joined by two women and another man. This was not a choreographed performance but spontaneous. Lubeles picked up the rifle and began to reenact the hunt. Several other men joined him. He bent forward, scanning and pointing the rifle, craning his neck and shading his eyes, and his feet never missed a beat. They performed the entire drama, sighting the elephant, creeping up to it, shooting and chasing, and finally butchering. Even the children were encouraged to participate."

An elephant bristling with spears and hunters dancing all around it. This is not the savagery that Livingstone describes or that Silas and other poachers participated in, but a ritual performed with reverence by men who knew how to pray. What I have seen in photographs of

African rock art Stuart witnessed in the firelight at Chanda's village. By his words he paints the scene before my eyes, as on a granite wall, and you can tell by the grunts and murmurs of the black men that his colors are true.

"Early the next morning Lubeles and I took the head meat, which they call nama shabwanga, and the stirring stick that had been used to cook it and went out in search of an elephant trail. I had left the party at about nine the night before, before the feasting began, but Lubeles told me that after all the meat was gone they had filled the pot it was cooked in with cold water, and everyone who had eaten washed his hands in it and then they poured it out in front of his father's hut. When we found a fresh elephant path, Lubeles dug a hole and placed the meat and a little nsima in it. That was to influence other elephants who passed that way to succumb to the hunter. After he covered up the hole, he threw the stirring stick off into the bush and said, 'We nama shala apa,' which means, 'You animal stay here.' And that was the end of it, except for what they call kulotesha, which means to continue dreaming of one thing, night after night, like elephants. When that happens, the hunter knows that it is time to go again."

As I LIE on the mattress in the moonlight, surrounded by protective fires, voices bear me into dreaming, men talking about hunting. The lion roars from the park, moving toward the bait. Steve and Stuart and Harry wait for him in the *machan,* armed and silent, but these men are talking, telling stories—Demetrius and Mbuluma and Silas the poacher, Karim the true African, and Stuart Marks who speaks their language and enters into their conversation. I wonder if Steve's satisfaction with the safari will depend on whether or not he kills the lion tonight. I know that would help. The trip has not been all that he has hoped or expected. He had been given to believe that he would get a chance at another buffalo, but the permit did not come through, and the leopard hunt has left a stench worse than the cat's actual odor. I know what it's like to want success, to want it so badly that you hang an entire enterprise on the outcome. If I had not killed the kudu, would I be feeling as good as I am? I doubt it. In any case,

I wanted it badly enough to understand what Steve is dealing with, and it's far more complicated than merely getting to take a trophy back to Georgia. Whatever happens between now and first light, neither of us would trade places right now with each other or with anyone else. In the strange tongue of these men and in their molded faces rendered timeless by the firelight, Africa has kept its promise to me.

A SHOT RANG OUT, penetrating sleep, shattering dream. I opened my eyes to a flurry of activity, people dashing back and forth in the moonlight. The mattress was all but jerked out from under me, rolled up, and stuffed into the back of the Land Cruiser, and then we were bouncing down the winding track, too fast, toward the bait and whatever had happened there.

Karim pulled up at the foot of the *machan*, headbeams fixed on the bush in front of us, and Demetrius flashed a spotlight in an arc around the area. A dead lion had to be out there somewhere, for Harry was laughing from the blind above our heads. But the light showed no lion.

As the eastern sky began to gray, Steve told the story. We were gathered around the Land Cruiser, some of us seated, others leaning against it. It had taken the lion half the night to come from the park to the bait, he said, but they had marked his progress by his roaring. Meanwhile, a pair of leopards had entertained them with courtship howlings just below the *machan*. They could not see the cats, but the growling and spitting and squalling went on for quite a while. Then the leopards fell silent and departed, knowing the lion was near. Instead of going straight to the bait, though, the lion circled the meadow, scent-marking the territory. It was a big animal, six or eight years old. They could see it in the moonlight. Then it settled down in long grass at the edge of the meadow and apparently went to sleep, for they heard no more from it until shortly before dawn. Steve said he himself had gone to sleep too, but he was awakened by the roar of the lion directly beneath them. Harry gripped his arm, and Steve peeped over the wall of the blind. The lion was walking across the opening to the bait. Steve took the rifle and found the lion in the scope. He had still not decided to shoot—he badly wanted to use his bow and he had envisioned the opportunity occurring at dawn—but his finger was on the trigger. What he saw screamed out at him. Harry spotted it through binoculars at the same instant and said, "No, don't shoot." The neck of the lion was laid open all the way around, cut by a wire snare. The lion had somehow managed to remove the loop but in the process had torn out most of his mane, leaving a collar of gaping red. He had been visiting the bait for at least a week but had not been able to stretch his neck far enough to reach it and feed.

"Do you think a taxidermist could fix that?" Steve whispered to Harry.

"No. Too much damage."

"Will he survive?"

"Hard to say."

THE REASON for Harry's laughter was his relief that Steve had not shot the lion. "I'm almost as glad as I would have been if Steve had gotten a good trophy," Harry told me.

"Why?"

"You just don't shoot a badly damaged animal. It doesn't look good."

"But wouldn't it have been an act of mercy? I mean, hyenas will get him sooner or later, won't they?"

"Probably, but we're going to lower the bait so he can eat. He might make it."

Steve would return home without a lion, the animal he had wanted most badly, but he was glad that the neck wound had kept him from shooting. A lion taken with a rifle at night was not what he had come to Africa for.

ON OUR LAST AFTERNOON we left the rifles and bows in camp and rode into the park and became bunny huggers. As Harry drove us through the Nsefu Sector on the east side of the river, we delighted in the illusion of the first Garden—a flock of crowned cranes sporting at a hot springs, a solitary bull elephant with long, heavy tusks, right beside the track, almost as safe from poachers as from safari hunters, pulling down acacia branches by the trunkful, and a herd of more than a thousand buffalo that Harry drove smack into the middle of. With their heavy bosses lifted all around us and wet black muzzles drooling long strings of saliva, Harry pulled up for us to get pictures. The vibration of the running vehicle kept Stuart and me from holding our cameras still, but Harry would not shut off the engine. Bold Stuart stepped out onto the ground with the video but Harry collared him. Too dangerous.

The immensity of sky above the open plain was smudged with columns of smoke. Throughout the valley, from the escarpment in the west to the hills in the east, game scouts were setting brush fires. As the sun went down behind the Muchingas, the sky turned to flame and the tall unraveling columns of smoke grew luminous with color.

Part Five

KULOTESHA

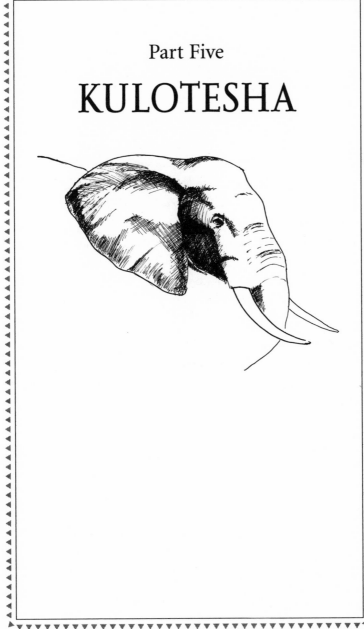

Kulotesha is an extension of the verb "to dream" and means "to continue dreaming one thing for a long time."
STUART MARKS, *Large Mammals and a Brave People*

All I wanted to do now was get back to Africa. We had not left it, yet, but when I would wake in the night I would lie, listening, homesick for it already.
ERNEST HEMINGWAY, *Green Hills of Africa*

During my first months after my return to Denmark from Africa, I had great trouble seeing anything at all as reality.
ISAK DINESEN, *Shadows on the Grass*

XI

▼▼▼▼▼

ON THE FRONT COVER of *The Last Journals of David Livingstone*, in both the British and American first editions, is a gilt-embossed image of the missionary being carried across a flooded river in a driving rain on the shoulders of his servant Susi. It is taken from a wood engraving that appears in the book above a quotation from the journal: "The main stream came up to Susi's mouth." Following Susi and Livingstone come the rest of the party, holding firearms above their heads. It was January 1873, the peak of the rainy season, and the Livingstone expedition of sixty African porters found themselves mired in the vast marshy expanses of the Bangweulu swamps of what is now central Zambia. It had been raining incessantly for weeks. Their canoes swamped when they crossed streams, soaking their gear, and they slept wet every night. After six weeks of unrelieved misery, Livingstone wrote in his journal, "A lion had wandered into this world of water and anthills, and roared night and morning, as if very much disgusted: we could sympathize with him!"

That Livingstone could generate even the little humor it took to make that entry is impressive. He was dying of dysentery, bleeding rectally, and the pain in his lower back and abdomen was almost unbearable. On March 19, his sixtieth birthday, he wrote, "Thanks to the Almighty Preserver of men for sparing me thus far on the journey of life. Can I hope for ultimate success? So many obstacles have arisen. Let not Satan prevail over me, oh! My good Lord Jesus!"

Scholars still debate what Livingstone meant by "ultimate success." In this, his final expedition, he was determined to find the source of the

Nile, a discovery by which he would outshine the explorers Richard Burton, John Hanning Speke, and Samuel Baker and recover his lost reputation, but, more importantly, according to Livingstone himself, he would gain sufficient influence in the chambers of government to bring about the end of the slave trade. "The Nile sources are valuable only as a means of enabling me to open my mouth with power among men. It is this power I hope to apply to remedy an enormous evil." Until that happened, he believed, there could be no hope of establishing Christianity in Africa. So it appears that Livingstone's motives, like those of any person, were an inseparable mixture—in his case an amalgam of ego, humanitarian zeal, religious devotion, and a passionate love of African country, flora, fauna, weather, and terrain.

In the mid-nineteenth century, as European powers began to stake claims in undeveloped parts of the globe, the location of the source of the Nile was the most compelling of all geographical mysteries. Burton and Speke had ventured in search of it in 1858 and became the first Europeans to reach Lake Tanganyika. While Burton was incapacitated by illness, Speke explored north and came upon the southern shore of a vast body of water he named Victoria Nyanza. This, he was certain, had to be the source of the Nile, but Burton later dismissed the claim with contempt. In 1862 Speke returned to Lake Victoria with James Grant and this time worked his way around to the north end where he found the outlet he expected. Upon his return to England two years later, he and Burton agreed to debate the issue at a meeting of the Royal Geographic Society at Bath. Livingstone was present, for the first time fascinated by the question, but the debate never took place. The day before, Speke died in a shooting accident that may have been suicide. When Sir Roderick Murchison of the RGS proposed to Livingstone that he go back to Africa to settle the question for good, he jumped at the opportunity.

By the fall of 1871 Livingstone had been wandering in the interior for more than four years, exploring and mapping the central African watershed. Reports of his death had reached England, and several expeditions had gone out in search of him. He, meanwhile, was facing one adversity after another—tribes that were either cowed or hostile because of the slave trade, rebellions and desertions among his own men, especially a group of sepoys from India, theft of supplies and loss of domestic animals, lack of food, and, as always, fever and dysentery. Reduced to dependence on Swahili slave traders, he regrouped at Ujiji, on the eastern shore of Lake Tanganyika, and it was there that he was found by the *New York Herald* journalist Henry Morton Stanley, who said, as he doffed his helmet to the doctor's lifted cap, "Dr. Livingstone, I presume?"

Stanley brought badly needed supplies, medicines, and porters. During the next five months, as Livingstone recovered his strength, the two men explored the Tanganyika region, developing in the process a kind of father-son relationship. At the end of that time, Stanley left for England and the fame and fortune he would win as the man who found Livingstone, but the missionary remained in Africa, more strongly determined than ever to locate the source of the Nile.

Livingstone had made a fatal error in discounting the conclusions of Speke and Grant. Ruling out Victoria Nyanza and Lake Albert, the true sources, he turned to the southwest, toward the Lualaba, with the intention of following that river north until it became the Nile. If he had had the time and strength to complete his plan, he would have discovered that the Lualaba becomes not the Nile but the Congo, but illness and weather kept him mired in the Bangweulu swamps, lost both literally and metaphorically.

But not spiritually. The sufferings of his last weeks seemed to produce in him a kinder spirit and a deeper faith. He was in constant agony and fearful that he would not live to complete his work, yet there is no record of his abusing even verbally the black men who were working for him. Day after day the party forged on through the vast flooded marsh, wading through water knee-deep and deeper, and when Livingstone could walk no further his men fashioned a tented stretcher and carried him carefully on their shoulders. The devotion and loyalty of these Africans—not only his personal servants Susi and Chuma but also the sixty recently hired porters—is testimony to the love Livingstone felt for them. Some scholars regard the image of the missionary—this champion of Christianity and commerce—straddling the shoulders of a black African crossing a flooded stream as an eloquent picture of colonial oppression, but the evidence suggests that Susi loved the man he served, and none of the many who remained loyal to him when they might easily have deserted had any reasonable hope of a monetary reward for their devotion. The simple explanation seems to be that this often irascible, cantankerous missionary, who had trouble getting along with other white men, treated Africans with kindness and respect, and they repaid him with their faithful service.

Even in these most discouraging of circumstances, Livingstone kept up his journal as long as he could hold a pencil, recording observations of the natural world: "I measured the crown of a papyrus plant, or palm: it was three feet across horizontally, its stalk eight feet in height. Hundreds of a large dark-gray, hairy caterpillar have nearly cleared off the rushes in spots and now live on each other." But on the nineteenth of April he wrote, "I am excessively weak, and but for the donkey, could not move a hundred yards. It is not all pleasure, this exploration. The Lavusi hills are a relief to the eye in this flat upland. Their forms show an igneous origin. . . . No observations now, owing to great weakness: I can scarcely hold a pencil, and my stick is a burden." Nevertheless, on the next day, a Sunday, he conducted what he called "service." Through the following week he made no entries at all, and then, on the twenty-seventh, he wrote for the last time: "Am knocked up quite."

He spent the next two or three days in agony. Unable even to stand, he was lifted, carried, ferried across rivers, and brought at last to an almost empty village, where his men laid him in a hut they had built for him. Susi and Chuma attended him through the evening of the thirtieth, but the missionary spoke little. Around midnight he dismissed Susi, "All right; you can go out now." At 4:00 a boy sitting with the sick man summoned Susi, who woke Chuma and four others. Together they entered the hut. Livingstone was kneeling at the side of the earthen embankment upon which they had made his bed, his body stretched forward and his head in his hands, as though he were praying. He had been dead for several hours.

Susi and Chuma may well have decided on their course of action already, for they went to work as soon as it was daylight, preparing the body of their master and friend for the fifteen-hundred-mile trek to the Indian Ocean and from there on to England—a dangerous as well as a difficult undertaking, for they would encounter tribes that considered corpses taboo and the handling of them witchcraft. First they removed the heart and other internal organs and buried them beneath an *mpundu* tree. In the process they discovered in the lower intestine a blood clot the size of a man's fist, surely the cause of Livingstone's unspeakable pain. One of the men, Jacob Wainwright, was literate; Susi suggested that he carve in the trunk the inscription "LIVINGSTONE, MAY 4, 1873" and the names of three important members of the party. Having preserved the corpse with salt and dried it fourteen days in the sun, they wrapped it in calico, placed it in a cylinder of bark, covered the cylinder with sailcloth, and smeared the cloth with tar. The journey, undertaken by the entire party of sixty men, took five arduous months. When they arrived in Zanzibar, an interim British official paid them meager wages out of his own pocket and sent them away. Only Wainwright was allowed to accompany the body to London, though a year later Livingstone's major benefactor bought passage to England for Susi and Chuma.

SEVERAL YEARS AGO Britain issued a set of commemorative stamps honoring great British explorers. In a gallery of portraits that includes Sir Francis Drake, Sir Walter Raleigh, and Sir Robert Falcon Scott, is David Livingstone, his face superimposed upon a green map of Africa. At about the same time, Zambia issued a set of six Livingstone commemoratives, the denominations representing Livingstone not only as an explorer and a missionary but also as a friend of

Africans. One stamp shows him attacking slave traders; another, discovering the Victoria Falls; another, ministering to the sick; another, teaching the Bible; another, greeting Stanley. By the standards of philatelic art, the Zambian stamps are crude, poorly drawn and garishly colored, but they remind me as the British stamp does not that David Livingstone is Exhibit A of whatever it is that Africa can do to people.

BY THE TIME we left Zambia I had developed a strong affinity for the famous missionary-explorer. In addition to superficial similarities—same age, same race, same faith—I was fascinated by the apparent paradox of his love of God and his passion for Africa. I sensed that in him the two things were not only reconciled but actually related. I suspected, in fact, that Livingstone's joy in Africa may well have been his most authentic expression of praise and worship, and if I could understand how, I might understand my own little experience. But all I could say for sure as I climbed aboard the commuter plane at the Mfuwe airport was that he had stayed and I was leaving.

▼ ▼ ▼

THE FLIGHT from Lusaka to Johannesburg to Atlanta took twenty hours. We landed in Atlanta at about 8:00 on the morning of June 23. Having slept little, I stumbled through customs in a catatonic state, but the face of my wife, just beyond the gate, woke me up. I was glad to see her, but the world of glass and gleaming steel, moving sidewalks, shuttle trains, and computer-generated voices left me addled, and I stayed addled all the way back to 345 Milledge Heights in Athens, where I crawled into my big four-poster and plunged into a deep sleep.

The telephone jangled me awake. A voice I failed to recognize said, "Jim? When did you get back?"

"Back?"

"From Africa."

"I'm afraid I don't recognize your voice."

"Jim. This is Maggie."

Maggie Epstein, a friend of ours, apparently calling for Jane. "Are you calling from Athens, Maggie?"

Maggie laughed. "Now Jim. Where else would I be calling from? I'm sorry I woke you up. Go on back to sleep. I'll try Jane later."

"No, no," I said. "I needed to wake up anyway. It's time to pack."

For a moment Maggie said nothing. Then, "Pack? Where are you going?"

"I'm going home, Maggie."

Another pause. "Jim, where are you?"

"I'm in Zambia. I thought you knew that."

"Then how did I reach you?"

It hadn't occurred to me to wonder. Genuinely surprised, I said, "I don't know. The man I'm hunting with has a satellite phone. Maybe that number is coded into our phone at home or something—some electronic glitch—I don't know."

"This is just so bizarre. Jane has been trying to reach you for a week, and I just dial your home number and get you in Africa. I can't believe it."

"I can't either."

Maggie reported this conversation to me later, as well as to many other people. My recollection of it is hazy, but she said I was so firmly anchored in Africa that I at last convinced her. I told her about the camp, the hunt, Harry and Karim, the animals. I told her that if it were not for missing my family I would be happy to stay there forever. After ten minutes, I said, "Maggie, I love talking with you, but this is an international call. It's costing you a bundle."

"Oh," she said, "that's all right. Tell me more. This is just so strange."

Robert Ruark once wrote, "All I want is someone who will listen to me talk about Africa." I had Maggie's interested ear, but, thinking I had gone on too long about myself, I asked about her husband Murray, how was he getting along?

"Oh, he's fine," she said, "but, Jim, I just can't get over this."

A car pulled up in the driveway. A door opened and closed, and the sound jarred me into a sliding and shifting of undefined planes of awareness. I told Maggie that Jane was just then driving up.

For a moment she made no response. Then she asked, "Jim, where are you?"

And I said, "Maggie, I'm not sure. I must be at home, this is my bed."

IT TOOK A LONG TIME to wake up. The sun-heated smell of animals seemed to linger in my beard, and once, sitting on the front porch in the morning, I caught myself listening for the calls of emerald-spotted doves. I hung the painted fabrics I had bought in Mfuwe, spent hours mounting photos in an album, and began reading a biography of David Livingstone. It would be a year before the kudu head was mounted and delivered, but I chose the place where I would hang it. Twice I dreamed that I was back on the bank of the Luangwa River. What I didn't do was write. To understand all that had happened and to find the shape that might make sense of it was daunting.

AND THEN, on the evening of July 4, two weeks after I got back, I cleared my throat and spit into the toilet. The sputum was red blood. The next day my pulmonologist scheduled a bronchoscopy for the following Tuesday. Until then I wouldn't know the cause—whether a simple broken blood vessel or any of several kinds of cancer, including metastasis of what I already had—but the possibilities made my feet turn cold. One night I dreamed about a chimney sweep in long tails and top hat using a chain to knock loose hardened carbon from the inside of a clogged flue.

Fear is a insidious adversary. By binding us to the future, it leaves us paralyzed for life in the present. At the same time it drains the past of meaning. After the blood I had no desire to write. Africa ceased to matter.

It was during those fraught days, between the blood and the bronchoscopy, that our daughter-in-law brought our granddaughter for a visit. Caroline was two and a half, just beginning to speak in sentences. One night her mother went out with friends, leaving us the happy task of getting the little one to bed. After we had tucked her in, read her a story, said her prayers, and kissed her goodnight, she patted the pillow next to hers and said, "Papa, sleep here." Papa stretched out. Then she said, "Nana, turn out the light."

When Jane had left the room, Caroline turned toward me and her sweet breath bathed my face. Never before had she been so trusting of me. In two minutes she was breathing deeply and peacefully. I put my arms around her and took advantage of the opportunity to pray for her. I asked simply that she might grow up safe and strong and happy and that the beauty of the Lord God rest upon her. Then it occurred to me to mention that I'd like to stick around to watch that happen. As I lay there in the dark room, dimly lit by a small night lamp, there came a response in King James English: "Take no thought for the morrow. The morrow will take care of itself. What you hold in your arms is the holy present. Seek me here, for I am nowhere else but now."

Through the weeks of radiation that followed, I meditated daily on that word, and it brought me a measure of peace. It also restored to me the vitality of my memories of Africa, and I saw that what I had experienced out there in the bush was the present, or the immanence of the present, which is not God but access to Him. The creation and the creatures in it, men and beasts, had enticed me into the now and held me there enthralled for three weeks as I had not been enthralled since childhood when I had no past and the future held no threat. And best of all, I saw that Africa had been a gift, freely given, no strings attached, no fine print—simply an opportunity to present myself to the present, every moment, moment by moment, whatever the present might bring. There was nothing religious about it, in the conventional sense of that word, but a cosmic energy that I am pleased to call the grace of God, which said, and still says, Here, this is for you. Be alive and enjoy.

As it happened, I had come home from Africa with more than I bargained for. At about the time I began radiation for the lesion in my chest, Steve came down with malaria—*falciperum,* the bad kind—and it almost killed him before prayer and quinine stopped it in its tracks. Mine was a milder strain. It didn't hit until October, but it was malaria all the same, my doctor said. A week of quinine, almost as bad as the disease, did strange things to my head. My ears rang constantly, drowning out all sound, and I wondered if what I really had was not malaria but a visitation of *chibanda,* the spirit of a slain animal that haunts the hunter who has failed to observe the proprieties. But I felt that I had handled the kudu with appropriate gratitude and admiration. If this was a visitation, it must be Africa itself, reminding me that I had not yet performed a *vizemba.* I had not celebrated the gift by dance and song, or, to change the metaphor, by dipping my brush into a pot of pigment and painting. But the time had come to begin.

ACKNOWLEDGMENTS

THE AFRICANS I MET in Zambia, especially on safari, treated me with unfailing kindness and respect. I have tried to reciprocate by changing their names in this narrative.

My friend Bob Benson and I have shared our dreams of Africa for many years. I wish he could have been with us at the timeless campfire. Ken Ware has opened to me his impressive collection of books about Africa and sustained an enthusiastic conversation about the history of African hunting. Stuart Marks has generously provided me access to his extensive research on Bisa culture and the animals of the Luangwa Valley. The best way of discharging the considerable debt I owe him is to represent as accurately as possible his careful and discerning work.

One of the great joys in seeing this book through to publication was the opportunity of working with the gifted editor Barbara Ras at the University of Georgia Press. The writers she has nurtured constitute a who's who of literary naturalists, and I count it a high honor to have my name appended to that list. She has made *Colors of Africa* a better book than it could possibly have been without her sharp eye, her keen ear, and her friendship.

As always, my wife, Jane, has listened patiently to every word and responded with great good sense to every extravagance. Her support, from the beginning of this African venture to the last written word, has been invaluable.